Questions and Answers

FRENCH

Steven Crossland

Principal Examiner

SERIES EDITOR: BOB McDUELL

EDUCATIONAL

Contents

HOW TO USE THIS BOOK

The aim of this book is to provide you, the student, with the help you need to reach the highest level of achievement possible at GCSE or, in Scotland, at General and Credit levels. The book is designed to help all students up to A* grade standard at GCSE.

The *Questions and Answers* series is based on the belief that experienced Examiners can provide, through examination questions, sample answers and advice, the help you need to secure success.

Students often find it useful to plan their revision according to some pattern during which weaknesses can be identified and eliminated so that confidence can grow. The primary consideration in devising these books, then, has been to present the main principles on which study can be based.

This *Questions and Answers* Guide is designed to provide:

● Brief **revision summaries** and hints on the examination in general, identifying the important information you must understand if progress is to be made answering examination questions. Spend some time on this section first and refer back to it whenever you find it necessary. There should not be anything in these sections which is brand new, but it is always useful to remind yourself of the important points about revision and examination procedure.

● **Advice** on each of the separate components or skill areas with hints on the different techniques required to perform to the highest standards. Notes are included about the nature of each different type of task that you are likely to encounter in the examination and guidance is given to enable you to gain practice at each stage.

● Many examples of **examination questions**. You will find that you will make progress by studying a wide range of questions and by heeding the guidance given on ways to improve or learn from answers given to these questions. The questions are taken from past papers of all the GCSE Examination Boards in Great Britain.

● **Sample answers** to questions on the Speaking and Writing components. Although not always perfect answers, they point the way forward for you and perhaps they challenge you to do better. You can try the questions for yourself before checking the sample answers and you can then go on to try the other examples given.

● **Answers** to the Listening and Reading exercises are also given at the back of the book.

● **Examiner's tips**. By using the experience of an Examiner you can gain advice which can enable you to see how your answers can be improved and hence ensure success.

● A **cassette** accompanying the book which contains material for the Speaking and Listening components. Details of this are given in the relevant sections of the book. Side One, Speaking, gives the teacher's part for the Role Plays and a large number of questions in French for you to practise, followed by sample answers, whilst the second side of the cassette contains the recorded material for the Listening exercises.

GCSE FRENCH – WHAT DO I HAVE TO KNOW?

Whichever GCSE French examination you take, the same basic language skills are tested. These skills are:

- Speaking – the ability to make yourself understood when speaking French.
- Listening – the ability to understand spoken French.
- Reading – the ability to understand written French.
- Writing – the ability to make yourself understood when writing French.

You don't have to be equally good at all these skills to be a good linguist, but normally competence in one skill area means competence in the others. At GCSE all four of these skills are tested to an equal degree – they have 'equal weighting' – and they are tested at a basic, or fairly easy level, and also at a higher, or more complex level. You can attempt each skill area at the level you choose, but only by succeeding at the higher levels can you be assured of obtaining a top grade. You must remember also that, although you are not in fact obliged to take the writing examination, you can not be awarded a grade higher than E unless you do so. It is also essential that candidates taking the MEG examination (which has three levels) remember that they **must** attempt Writing up to Higher Part 2 in order to reach Grade B or better.

It's important to remember that you are not expected to be able to speak and write faultless French in order to get a good GCSE grade. After all, who speaks and writes their own language without error? No-one. The important thing, in speaking and writing any language is **to be understood** or to **communicate** with reasonable clarity.

As for understanding written and spoken French (i.e. reading and listening comprehension), once again it is not necessary to be perfect – you are not expected to understand every single word. A very important skill in language is 'gist' comprehension – i.e. you understand the general idea of a passage of written or spoken French by being able to pick out certain words or phrases. There are pitfalls here, however – it is easy to misunderstand a sentence because, even though you are familiar with a number of words in it, you miss a key word such as a negative or the particular tense of a verb.

At Higher Level, 'gist' understanding is tested to a greater depth and greater accuracy is expected in writing and speaking. You need to do well in your Basic Level papers (you usually need to score about 75% or more to be sure of maximum points) but you need to be successful at Higher Level in order to achieve the top grades.

TOPICS AND SETTINGS

It is useful if you can obtain a copy of the syllabus or the 'Defined Content' for the examination for which you will be entered. As well as giving an outline of the topics you need to be familiar with, the Defined Content lists all the grammar structures and all the different French words that you are expected to know – indeed, you will not be tested on your knowledge of any word which does not appear in the vocabulary lists which each Examination Board must publish.

The lists of words vary slightly from one Board to another, but the topics tend to be the same for each. Check that you have learned the vocabulary and are able to write and speak about the following topic areas:

Personal identification.
Family, friends and social interaction.
House and home.
Daily routine.
Geographical surroundings – town and country.
School.

Hobbies, free time, sport and entertainments.
Travel, public and private transport.
Shopping.
Food and drink.
Holidays.
Accommodation (hotels, campsites, youth hostels etc.).
Weather.
Health and welfare (illness, emergencies, the chemist's).
Work, education and future plans.
Services (bank, post office, tourist office, lost property office, the police).

Sometimes you will have items in the examination that do not appear to fit neatly into any of the above topic areas, but they will normally be associated with one or more of these.

To find out what types of exercises you are likely to come across in the examination – read on! Within each section there is a range of exercises taken from different Examination Boards. At the start of each section you will find the Basic, Elementary or Foundation Level exercises. These lead on to the more demanding exercises that are set at Higher, Extended or Credit Level.

GENERAL REVISION HINTS

The best way to practise for your GCSE examination is to speak French whenever you can. It doesn't matter whether you speak to a friend, a brother, sister or other relative who is prepared to listen to you or to yourself, because the most important thing in making progress in a foreign language is **confidence**.

You will find more particular advice about practising your speaking in Section 1 on page 6. But practice in speaking French will give you greater confidence in all aspects of the language. It's not the only thing to practise, obviously, but it's perhaps the easiest – you don't need to have books, it doesn't really matter where you are (in the bath, while taking the dog for a walk, on the way to school) because all you have to do is to talk in French about yourself, the things that interest you, what you did the other day, what you're going to do that day and so on.

You need to revise the grammar and the vocabulary of French on a regular basis. Try to arrange a revision programme that you stick to during the months leading up to the exam. You don't need to do hours every night – just try and do a regular revision slot. It will depend on the text book that you have where you find the information, but most books give a list of the grammar points covered. If you don't have a text book, see if your teacher will loan you one or find a suitable book in the library (though it's still best to ask your teacher's advice about the book you find). Test yourself or your friends on the vocabulary once you've covered a particular topic in your revision programme. There are some quite inexpensive books for sale which contain lists of key words for GCSE French – your teacher may have already told you about them, but ask for advice if you need it.

Asking for help from your French teacher during the year is a very important revision device. Your teacher wants you to succeed and, as long as you ask politely and at a convenient time the chances are he or she will be only too willing to help. At the same time, your teacher will no doubt be giving you plenty of advice during the lessons. Make sure you note it! If your teacher gives you vocabulary sheets, grammar revision notes, sample role plays etc. keep them together neatly. Use a document wallet or a file to keep your notes in. Listen carefully in class and let the teacher know if you don't understand a particular point (don't be shy about doing this – your teacher and others in the class will probably respect you for doing so).

When a piece of homework involving written French is returned to you (a letter for instance) check to see where you have made any mistakes. The teacher may or may not have underlined each error – he or she will no doubt have explained to you how the marking has been done – but you need to find out what mistakes you have made and why (see the Writing section on page 50 for more hints about this). Make a note of the mistake, write down what it should have been and do your best to avoid making the same mistake in the future (some mistakes are very common and keep on occurring. Try to make sure that **you** don't make them!).

Keep a note of any new words that come up (but be careful to note them correctly). Even though you might be able to find the word in a dictionary or vocabulary list it's still a good idea to write it down for yourself (writing it down helps you to remember it). And if you can then use the word in speaking or writing you will find it sticks much more easily in your memory. Note the words in a small note book for use as a vocabulary book. Keep it carefully though – it's easy to mislay!

As you approach the exam you will probably have the chance to study past exam papers. This is a very useful source of practice and you will find plenty of examples with which to practise in this book. Although identical questions never come up from one year to the next, they follow a similar pattern and the more you see, the more familiar you will become with the style of questions. It is quite likely that very similar Role Plays in the Speaking test will reappear after a few years. After all, there's only a limited number of Role Play topics that you are expected to have covered and the examination setters try to keep standards similar from one exam to the next. If your teacher lets you keep copies of past papers, keep them safely in your file and use them for exam practice. Study the style of questions used in the Reading and Listening and note how, on Higher Level papers, the wording of questions becomes more complex. Go through the Role Plays that have been set and re-do them with minor variations. Do the same for the Writing tasks – change the details of time or date or place so that you can practise the question with slight variations – it will all help to give you practice and confidence.

This book will give you plenty of examples of exam questions to practise. Work through them at regular intervals, check the answers in the back and study the sample answers. Keep practising, stay confident – and good luck for the exam!

REVISION CHECKLIST

In order to help with your revision for the examination, you may find it useful to check that you have covered the points below. Do remember that this is only a very general checklist; you need also to refer to more detailed grammar summaries such as you will find in the back of your school text book or in the *Letts GCSE French Study Guide*.

You should, however, make sure that you have covered the following thoroughly:

- **Key vocabulary** relating to the topics set out on pages 2–3 above. For example: school subjects, forms of transport, holiday activities, common drinks and snacks, weather etc.
- **Numbers**: all of them! Remember to be familiar with the sound as well as the sight of them (i.e. they need to be recognised in listening as well as in reading). Learn in particular the numbers 12–16, 70–80 and 90–100. Be clear of the difference in sound between *deux*, *dix* and *douze*. Don't forget to learn basic 'ordinal' numbers (*premier*, *deuxième* etc.).
- **Times**.
- **Days**. **Months**. **Dates**.
- **Seasons** (e.g. *été*) and **festivals** (e.g. *Pâques*).
- **Directions** (*à gauche* etc.) and **positions** (*près de*, *à côté de*, *devant* etc.).
- **Countries** and **nationalities** (e.g. *Allemagne*; *allemand*).
- **Question Words**: *qui*; *quel/quelle/quels/quelles*; *où*; *quand*; *combien*; *comment*; *pourquoi*; *qu'est-ce que*; *est-ce que*; *lequel* (*laquelle* etc.).
- **Descriptions** of people and things; learn the rules of adjective agreement (*les yeux bleus*; *une petite voiture*).
- **Phrases to describe feelings, opinions and emotions** (e.g. *j'étais déçu(e)*; *c'était ennuyeux*; *je pense que c'est formidable*; *j'ai peur* etc.).

Verbs

You must be familiar with the use of verbs in the following tenses:

(Note: examples given below are all in the first person singular (i.e. *je*) forms. You should also be able to use the other forms, in particular *il/elle/on*; *nous* and *ils*.)

Present: *je mange*; *je vais*; *je me lève*; *je n'aime pas*.

Perfect: *j'ai joué*; *j'ai vu*; *je suis allé(e)*; *je suis parti(e)*; *je me suis reposé(e)*; *je n'ai pas décidé*.

Future: EITHER: *je vais passer*; *je ne vais pas travailler, je vais me coucher.*
OR: *je passerai*; *je ne travaillerai pas*; *je me coucherai.*

Imperfect: *je faisais*; *j'habitais*; *j'étais*; *j'allais*; *je n'avais pas*; *je me détendais*.
And N.B. *il faisait* (for weather), *c'était* (it was) and *il y avait* (there was/were).

You will also have used the **conditional** tense (e.g. 'I would buy'). Use the future stem and add the imperfect ending (*j'achèterais*).

It is also quite easy, and good style, to use the **pluperfect** tense (e.g. 'I had lost'). Form this as for the perfect tense but use the **imperfect** tense forms of *avoir* (or *être*) – e.g. *j'avais perdu*; *j'étais retournée*.

LEARN the following irregular **perfect tense** forms:

AVOIR – *j'ai eu* (I have had) BOIRE – *j'ai bu* (I drank)
COURIR – *j'ai couru* (I ran) DEVOIR – *j'ai dû* (I had to)
DIRE – *j'ai dit* (I said/told) ÉCRIRE – *j'ai écrit* (I wrote)
ÊTRE – *j'ai été* (I have been) FAIRE – *j'ai fait* (I did/made)
LIRE – *j'ai lu* (I have read) METTRE – *j'ai mis* (I have put)
NAÎTRE – *je suis né(e)* (I was born) OUVRIR – *j'ai ouvert* (I opened)
PLEUVOIR – *il a plu* (it rained) POUVOIR – *j'ai pu* (I have been able);
PRENDRE – *j'ai pris* (I took) RECEVOIR – *j'ai reçu* (I received);
(SOU)RIRE – *j'ai (sou)ri* (I smiled/laughed) VENIR – *je suis venu(e)* – I came;
VOIR – *j'ai vu* (I saw)

LEARN the list of verbs that use *être* in the perfect (and pluperfect) tense:

ALLER PARTIR
ARRIVER RENTRER
DESCENDRE RESTER
ENTRER RETOURNER
MONTER SORTIR
MOURIR TOMBER
NAÎTRE VENIR (DEVENIR; REVENIR)

LEARN the **imperfect/conditional tense** endings:
je/tu … ais; *il/elle/on … ait*; *nous …ions*;
vous …iez; *ils/elles …aient*.

LEARN the **future tense** endings:
je … ai; tu … as; il/elle/on … a;
nous … ons; vous … ez; ils/elles … ont.

REVISION HINTS

Confidence in speaking French is the key to success in the other skills, and confidence comes from regular practice. You don't have to be in class to practise speaking French – you don't even have to be with anyone else! Decide to speak French to yourself on your way to school or on a Sunday afternoon, for instance. Agree to chat French with a friend preparing for the exam with you.

The oral exam will always include a **General Conversation** section in which you are asked questions about everyday topics such as: yourself and your family, your home, your town or village, your interests or pastimes, your school and your holidays. You may also be asked about things that you have done – how you spent the weekend, the last holidays, any visits to France – where obviously your skill in using the past tense is being tested. Or, to test your competence with expressing the future you may be asked what you plan to do next weekend, during the next holidays, after the exams or as a career. These, then, are the kinds of topics that you should practise talking about.

You will also have to perform **Role Plays** in French. In order to practise for this, imagine yourself in those situations which you have worked on during your French studies – in a shop, a café, a restaurant, a station, a tourist office etc. And remember to practise talking about awkward situations or complaining – the car has broken down, the chips are cold, you've lost your wallet etc.

EXAM HINTS

Speak French to yourself on the day of the examination as soon as you get up. Report for the examination on time. Avoid having to rush at all costs. You will probably feel nervous but you must remember that your teacher wants you to do well and may be nervous as well! Use your preparation time wisely by talking through your part of the Role Plays quietly. Don't worry about a particular word that you might not know in a Role Play but think how you can best convey the idea. There are likely to be some words that you don't know anyway. Don't worry if you make some mistakes – everybody does. Don't be afraid to restart a sentence if you get into difficulties but remember that you can be given no credit for any answers given in English!

Role Plays

In a Role Play you follow instructions as if you were in a particular situation in France.

Usually the situation involves some sort of 'transaction', i.e. you are buying something in a shop or café, or booking in at a hotel, or asking for information at a station, tourist office etc. Your teacher or examiner plays the part of the salesperson or assistant.

Sometimes you have to imagine that you are in a situation with a pen-friend or exchange partner and are discussing something such as where to go or what to do. In this case, your teacher plays the part of the French pen-friend or partner.

Tu or *Vous?*

It is important to remember that, in the 'transactional' type of Role Play, where you are talking with someone whom you don't really know, you **must** use *vous* when addressing that person. This is the formal word used in French for 'you' when talking with a stranger. In the second type of Role Play when you are addressing a pen-friend or partner, it is obviously more appropriate to use the *tu* or informal word for 'you'. This is probably the form you will use with your teacher in the conversation section of the oral.

Right or Wrong?

Remember that the object is to convey the message on each task. Your teacher/examiner will give you credit as long as he or she thinks that a French person would understand what you say.

If you need to revise this subject more thoroughly, see the relevant topics in the *Letts* GCSE *French Study Guide.*

ROLE PLAYS

When you are ready, listen to **Side 1 of the cassette**. For each separate Role Play you will first hear the teacher/examiner's questions with spaces for you to record your role. Then you will hear a complete version with both roles. Listen to this so that you can check how you did. If you made any mistakes, have another go later.

Here are three short Role Play tasks at Basic Level to get you started. Remember that you have a few minutes to prepare them before you start, but that you are not allowed to look up words in a dictionary.

1 You are at a cinema box-office. Your teacher will play the part of the assistant and will start the conversation.

   (a) Ask for two tickets please.
   (b) Ask the box-office attendant to repeat that.
   (c) Say number 4 and ask what time the film starts.

2 You are talking with your pen-friend about holidays. Your teacher will play the part of your pen-friend and will start the conversation.

   (a) Say you are going to the seaside.
   (b) Say in three weeks.
   (c) Ask if your pen-friend is going by train.

3 You are at a petrol station. Your teacher will play the part of the attendant and will start the conversation.

   (a) Ask the attendant to fill the tank.
   (b) Say what type of fuel you want.
   (c) Ask if the attendant can check your tyres.

NEAB 1994

The next two examples are still at Basic Level, but in each case there are five tasks to perform instead of three.

   Again, listen to the cassette and speak your role during the pauses, then listen to the sample versions that follow. Try them again later if you made any mistakes.

A You visit a *café* in France with your pen-friend. Your teacher will play the part of the waiter/waitress.

   1 Order two ham sandwiches.
   2 Ask for two teas.
   3 Ask if there are any cakes.
   4 Say you would like two ice-creams.
   5 Say you will have strawberry ices.

B You arrive with a friend at a French youth hostel and speak to the warden.
  Your teacher will play the part of the warden.

   1 Ask if there is any room.
   2 Say it is for four nights.
   3 Ask the cost.

4   Ask for a sleeping bag.
5   Ask if there is an evening meal.

MEG 1994

> **Examiner's tip** Don't panic if you forget a basic word like 'strawberry'. In any case, when you are asked *quel parfum?*, you could always ask what flavours are available: *Quels parfums avez-vous?* Remember the useful phrase *il y a de la place?* for asking if there is room. It's also the word to use for a seat in a train, bus, cinema etc.

ROLE PLAY C Finally, two more Role Plays at Basic or General Level, that look a little more complex than the others. However, if you prepare them carefully you won't find them too difficult.

1   Whilst staying in France you ring up a restaurant. The examiner will play the part of the person who answers the phone. You speak first. Your tasks are:

(a) To ask to reserve a table for this evening.
(b) To say how many it is for.
(c) To say you will arrive at 8 p.m.
(d) To give your name and spell it.
(e) To say thank you and goodbye.

SEG 1993

> **Examiner's tip** Note that in this case **you** start the conversation, so have the first task prepared carefully. Task (c) looks as if it requires the future tense, but bear in mind that the French often use the present tense to talk about the future. Task (d) requires you to spell your name – using the French pronunciation of the letters obviously! Be sure you have learned how to spell your name in French.

2   Whilst on holiday in France, you lose a wallet. You go to the Police Station. The examiner will play the part of a policeman/woman. You speak first. Your tasks are:

(a) To greet the policeman/woman.
(b) To say what you have lost.
(c) To describe it very briefly.
(d) To ask what you should do.
(e) To ask where the Lost Property Office is.

SEG 1993

> **Examiner's tip** You need the past tense in task (b). You must know the word *porte-feuille* – there's no real way round it, though you could try *porte-monnaie*. To describe it simply you could refer to its size or colour or material. It's useful to learn the phrase *Que faire?*, needed in task (d). Finally note that, if you have forgotten *bureau des objets trouvés* in task (e) it probably doesn't matter because you would have been advised to go there in the answer to task (d). So all you need is *C'est où?*

Don't forget that the versions on the cassette are only samples and that there are usually several correct ways of expressing the tasks.

At the more advanced levels of the examination, Role Plays become more demanding in the following ways:

● Tasks are more complex and will often include more than one element.
● There may be more tasks than at Basic Level.
● Knowledge of Higher Level vocabulary will be tested.
● Some tasks will be unprepared; that is, you will not know what is required until your teacher asks the question. The instruction on your card will simply be something like: 'answer the employee's next question'.
● You may be required to express an appropriate emotion such as disappointment or anger.

You should spend longer on preparing Role Plays at this level – you shouldn't find the Basic Level Role Plays too difficult anyway, so you can concentrate on the Higher Level. Try to predict what the unprepared question might be and work out how you can get round any problems of vocabulary. Usually there will be more than one mark per task available, so you can gain credit for partially correct responses, though as in all Role Plays, marks are awarded on the basis of how well you would be understood by a French person.

ROLE PLAY D

You have arrived at a hotel in Paris. The examiner will play the part of the receptionist.

1 Give your surname and say that you have a reservation.
2 Explain that you telephoned the hotel two weeks ago.
3 Say what kind of room you asked for. Give **two** details.
4 Say that you would like to stay for four nights.
5 Answer both parts of the receptionist's question.
6 Ask if it is easy to get to the Eiffel Tower.
7 Say you would like to walk there.

ULEAC 1994

Examiner's tip   Don't forget how to use the phrase *il y a* to express the idea of 'ago'. Be prepared to listen out for two questions for task **5**. For task **7**, remember that *aller à pied* is just as good as *marcher* to express 'to walk'. As a rule, avoid using the verb *se promener*.

ROLE PLAY E

As at Basic Level, you may have a Role Play in which you have a conversation with a pen-friend. Try this example:

You have just arrived at your pen-friend's home in Saumur. The examiner will play the part of your pen-friend.

1 Say that you enjoyed the journey to Saumur.
2 Answer your pen-friend's question, giving **two** details.
3 Ask what there is to see in the town.
4 Find out what you are going to do tomorrow.
5 Describe your home town to your pen-friend. Give **two** details.
6 Ask if you will be able to visit the castle in Saumur.
7 Ask your pen-friend what he/she usually does at weekends.

ULEAC 1994

Notice that two of the tasks require two details and that in the first instance it involves the unprepared task, so listen carefully for both questions. You need to be careful to use the correct tenses in this Role Play; note where the past, the present and the future tenses are needed. Don't forget, however, that it is quite natural to express the idea of the future with the present tense, e.g. *qu'est-ce qu'on fait demain?* for task **4**.

ROLE PLAY F Higher Level Role Plays are sometimes based on feeling unwell. This is a topic that you should revise for the oral. Here is an example for you to practise:

You visit a chemist's shop in France.
Your teacher will play the part of the chemist.

1 Tell the chemist that you do not feel very well.
2 Say you have a sore throat.
3 Give the information requested.
4 Ask if it is 'flu.
5 When given tablets, ask how many per day you should take.

MEG 1994

Examiner's tip In preparing this situation, you might be able to make a reasonable assumption about what the unprepared question will be (how long have you had the sore throat), but be prepared for it to be something else! Remember how to express the idea of 'I should' in task **5**. You can use the phrase *je dois* or *il faut* (both phrases followed by another verb in the infinitive) making your voice go up in order to form a question.

ROLE PLAY G The more difficult Higher Level Role Plays leave you to do the negotiation. You sometimes have to decide parts of the situation yourself and again, there will be unpredictable elements that will test how well you can make an immediate response rather than one that you have had time to prepare.

SITUATION
You have bought some jeans but decide to take them back to the shop. Your teacher will play the part of the shop assistant and will start the conversation.

YOU MUST

– Say you bought a pair of jeans and when you bought them.
– Say why you are bringing them back.
– Ask if you can try another pair.
– Respond appropriately to what the assistant tells you.

NEAB 1994

Examiner's tip Note that there are two elements to the first task and that both require the past tense. You may find that you don't know the verb 'to bring back', but think of verbs you know that would fit this situation – you could use a simpler verb such as *rendre* or even *donner* or you could think about using a phrase like *je ne veux pas ce jean parce que...* As always, the object is merely to express clearly in French the idea outlined in the English.

Letts
Q&A

NARRATOR ROLE PLAYS

As you approach the most difficult part of the oral exam, you start to play the part of a narrator telling about something that you experienced or witnessed. This will require use of the past tenses and you must obviously be confident in the use of both the **perfect** and the **imperfect** – the perfect to describe completed actions and the imperfect for description or for things that **were** happening at a given time.

ROLE PLAY H

Here is an example for you to practise. It is not possible to give a paused version on the cassette as you do most of the talking (but remember that your teacher is required to take part in a conversation about the events with you), but you will hear a short sample version which covers the main points.

While you were on holiday in France last year, you got stuck for four hours in this traffic jam on the motorway going south. Some time later you show this photograph to a French friend, and tell him/her about it.

     Remember to say   WHO was involved,
                         WHERE and WHEN it happened, and WHY,
                         WHAT happened and WHAT was said,
                         as well as giving any other details you care to make up about what
                         happened earlier or later.

The examiner will play the part of your friend, and is likely to interrupt you from time to time to ask you questions.

N.B. A traffic jam = un embouteillage **or** un bouchon

SEG 1994

ROLE PLAY I

And a final example for you to practise and then listen to. Note how the different past tenses are used, with the imperfect for description of the flat and the lost child and the perfect for all completed actions.

The notes below give details of an incident during a holiday spent in France with your family. You were staying in a rented flat and visited a supermarket to stock up on supplies. Back at school, you tell the *Assistant/e* about the shopping expedition.

Your teacher will play the part of the *Assistant/e*.

You need not mention every detail given in the notes, but you should try to make your account as full as possible.

1 arrivée en France	**2 au supermarché**
louer un appartement – grand?	décider d'acheter des provisions
petit?	laisser la voiture au parking
comment était-il?	acheter quoi - à manger? à boire
dans quelle région de la France?	chercher des légumes? des fruits? des vins?
avec quels membres de la famille?	
pour passer combien de temps?	

3 au rayon des disques	**4 un enfant perdu**
écouter des disques – de qui?	revenir au parking – voir un petit enfant
passer combien de temps?	où exactement? comment était-il?
acheter des cassettes – payer à la caisse	que faisait-il?
aller prendre quelque chose au restaurant	rentrer dans le magasin chercher la mère
	qu'est-ce qui s'est passé enfin?

MEG 1994

GENERAL CONVERSATION

Now you will hear on the cassette some questions (about 100 in fact!) to practise for the General Conversation section of your oral exam. Whatever exam syllabus you are preparing for, you will be required to answer questions of this type. Concentrate on giving brief, accurate answers to the questions. However, you should always aim to answer in a full sentence and be as accurate as you can. It is not expected that your pronunciation will be perfect, but you should avoid pronouncing words with an English accent and you can not be awarded any marks for answering a question wholly in English. Obviously you will sometimes use English if giving the name of your favourite TV programme or pop star, but you must include French in your answer by saying, for example: *Mon chanteur favori est...*

A short pause has been left after each question for you to give your answer, but you may prefer to pause the cassette longer in order to think or to give a more complex answer. After the pause for your answer, you will hear a sample answer to the same question.

Practise the questions on a regular basis, taking one topic in each session. Listen carefully to the model answers and see if your answers follow the same pattern.

The questions are grouped in eight topics as follows:

- Personal identity – self and family.
- House, home and geographical surroundings.
- Daily routine at home.
- Interests and pastimes.
- School.
- Past events.
- Holidays.
- Future plans.

EXTENDED CONVERSATION

Now you will have some practice talking on the above topics at length rather than simply answering each separate question individually – this is the Extended Conversation that is used by Exam Boards at Higher Level.

You will simply hear a general question on a particular topic to get you started. Once you hear the 'starter question', stop the cassette and try to talk for a minute or two about the subject. Again, practise this on a regular basis, taking one subject at a time.

Remember that in the exam, however, your teacher will make a conversation about the subject by asking questions during your talk. The idea is not that you should recite a learnt speech, but that you should be able to link up sentences and answer any questions your teacher might include.

After the ten Extended Conversation questions, you will hear sample conversations on three topics. Note how the speaker deals with the examiner's questions. Note too how the speaker is not 'word perfect' – she sometimes hesitates a little or restarts a sentence. It is therefore perfectly alright for you to do the same! But try to fill in your pauses with French words or 'grunts' – don't say 'um', say *euh!*. Listen how the French speaker fills in the pauses, and try to practise including appropriate fill-in words and phrases, which, although they mean very little, sound very French!

Here are some useful fill-in words and phrases:

alors!	*ben!*	*enfin!*
eh bien!	*tu vois!*	*euh!*

2 Listening

REVISION HINTS

You need as much practice as you can get in listening to French. Obviously you will have the chance to practise in class by listening to your teacher and to recordings. But you should try to find the time to listen to French at other times.

It's easy enough to tune in to French radio. Reception is generally better in the evenings. Try listening to France Inter on LW160 khz or Europe 1 on 180 khz. You'll be able to pick up others depending on where you live.

Don't get depressed when you discover that you can't understand much of the French that is being said! Reception is not particularly good – and they do seem to speak very fast! But it's useful to listen and try to pick out words or get the general gist of what is being said. And remember that the more practice you get in listening, the more your comprehension skills will improve.

There are opportunities to hear French spoken on British television as well. Usually when French films are shown, they are sub-titled. Many other programmes showing a French person talking have the English version of the words shown on the screen. It is useful practice to listen to the French and follow the English, but don't expect the one to be an exact translation of the other and don't be surprised if they seem to miss out some of it – after all, they don't want to fill up the whole screen with the translation!

Finally, try to arrange from time to time to speak French with your friends who are also preparing for the exam. By talking French with others you will be gaining extra practice in listening as well as in speaking. If by any chance you have a French pen-friend or exchange partner, ask him or her to send you a taped message in French or to make some recordings from French radio or TV for you. And of course, if you are lucky enough to be able to visit France, whether on a trip or exchange, you will have a marvellous opportunity to listen to French being spoken in all sorts of situations. Make the most of it!

See the Revision summary for Reading on page 28 for hints on learning vocabulary.

EXAMINATION HINTS

On the day of the Listening exam, practise talking French to yourself or your friends as you go to the exam. There is not a lot of point in reading through sheets of vocabulary lists at this stage, but getting yourself accustomed to speaking and hearing the language on the day of the exam will be helpful.

Read all questions and instructions carefully. You will have been told this many times by your teacher and the notes on the examination paper will remind you about it, but it is vitally important. As you read the questions, be alert to exactly what is being asked for. Don't read too quickly. It's surprising how easy it is, particularly when under exam stress, to read a 'When?' as a 'Where?'. It is sometimes useful, when reading the questions, to underline the key words in order to avoid errors (e.g. 'give **two** reasons for her answer'; 'what does he say he **doesn't** like about the holidays?').

Make use of the time given for reading and answering the questions. Never rush. Even for the easy Basic Level questions, use the time given for reading and answering wisely. You would be very annoyed if you found out later that you had missed part of an answer by rushing.

Listen to all playings. You will normally hear the French texts two or three times. Don't ignore the later playings. Very often something which is not clear on the first listening will become clearer when you hear it the second time. Even if you are confident that you have the answer from the first playing, listen anyway to subsequent playings – you may discover that you had misheard it. In any case you will use any later playings to check your answers carefully.

Make sure you can hear the recording. If you can not hear the tape as clearly as you should be able to, it is most important that you let the invigilator know at the very start of the exam (during the example question, for instance, if one has been recorded). You must not allow yourself to be put off, for example, by the continuous noise of a lawn-mower outside. It is up to you to let the invigilator know if there is anything that might be affecting your ability to hear the tape as clearly as possible.

Answer the questions fully – and legibly. This applies equally to the Reading paper. When you have written your answer, check that it is a full answer to the question (though never write more than is required by the question). Is your answer clear? Have you shown that you have understood the French? Will the examiner know what you mean? Will the examiner be able to read what you have written? If you have changed your answer, will the examiner know which one to mark?

Write no more than one answer to a question. It is not a good idea to hedge your bets and give more than one answer to a question. Some Exam Boards may award the mark if the correct answer appears, others may award it if your **first** answer is the correct one, others may forfeit the mark if any wrong answer appears with the correct one.

Take care not to 'invalidate' your answer. It is unlikely, particularly on the Higher Level papers, that you will gain a mark if, having answered a question correctly, you then proceed to include an incorrect detail. Do be careful, then, not to spoil a good answer by misunderstanding a simple detail such as a number. You can't always know, obviously, how much you should include in your answer, but the best advice is to be concise but thorough – in other words, answer what the question is asking for and no more.

Base your answers on what you hear. Although you will sometimes be asked on the Higher Level papers to draw conclusions and state your opinion, always remember that the purpose of the exam is to test your understanding of spoken French so don't waffle or guess answers. Draw your conclusions or base your opinions solely on the text that you have heard.

> If you need to revise this subject more thoroughly, see the relevant topics in the *Letts* GCSE *French Study Guide*.

BASIC **LISTENING QUESTIONS**

On the Basic or Elementary Level papers, you are generally asked to pick out individual items such as numbers, days, times, prices, details of people's likes and so on and to write them down in English or in figures. Sometimes you have to match up written statements with what you hear or take your pick from alternatives.

The detail you are listening out for will usually be quite clear and will often be followed by a pause on the tape for you to write your answer. You sometimes have to listen to a little more and perhaps then write more than one answer but, although you must not waste time, you should not find that you are too rushed to write down your answers.

Usually at the start of the test there will be a few short items in which you have to listen out for a particular detail (the question will make it quite clear what you are listening for). The French here is often in the form of announcements or instructions.

> N.B. In order to give plenty of examples on this cassette, each French sentence or text in these Basic Level exercises is played **once** only and pauses for writing answers have sometimes been reduced. You should note that you will usually hear the French stimulus **twice** in the examination. Rewind the cassette and play the sentence or exercise again in order to hear it for a second time. However, to give you an idea of what the exam is like, listen to each stimulus no more than twice.

LISTENING A

Here are a few examples. **You should be at the start of Side 2 of the cassette**. First, read the questions below.

1 You ask an official at the port which bus to take to the town centre. Which number bus are you told to take?

   .... (1)

2 You ask the driver how much the bus journey costs. How much is it?

   .... (1)

3 You have had a snack in a café and you ask for the bill. The waiter gives you the bill and tells you something. What does he tell you?

   .... (1)

4 Next you go shopping in the market. First you buy some grapes and the stall-holder tells you how much they cost. How much are they?

   .... (1)

5 You go to another stall and try on a hat. The stall-holder says something to you. What does he mean?

   .... (1)

   MEG 1994

The next five examples, although still at a fairly simple Basic Level standard, are slightly more difficult than the first five, either because they contain two separate items to answer or because the key word does not come right at the end of the sentence, thus making the listening skill a little more demanding.

LISTENING B

1 Once you get into town you go to a café. You order a drink and ask what snacks they have. Name **two** of the snacks the waiter suggests.

.... (2)

2 You ask where the toilets are. Where exactly are they?

.... (2)

3 You hear an announcement over the public address system about a fair in the town. **When** will the fair be taking place?

.... (1)

4 You are told that they do not serve the evening meal on one day of the week. Which day is this?

.... (1)

5 Soon after, you hear an announcement about a special offer. What item is on special offer and for how long will the offer last?

Item on offer .... (1)

Offer lasts .... (1)

MEG 1994

You may have to enter details on a form. Listen to this example where you must write down school subjects on a timetable. Then try the question that follows, where the girl expresses her opinion.

LISTENING C

Your friend Chantal is telling you about her school.

She is telling you her timetable for Tuesday, a typical school day, and you are writing it down so that you can compare it with your own school day.

Fill in the details of your friend's timetable:

	8.00	English		LUNCH	
(a)	9.00	....	(c)	2.00	....
(b)	10.00		(d)	3.00	....
	11.00	....	(e)	4.00	....
	12.00				

(5)

Now she tells you what she thinks about Tuesdays.

Tick the sentence which gives her opinion.

Tuesday is her best day. ☐

Tuesday is not too bad. ☐

She hates Tuesdays. ☐ (1)

ULEAC 1994

LISTENING D You are often required to take notes on a recorded message. Here is a short example.

Your pen-friend rings up to tell you the details of his arrival.

1 Where will he arrive?

.... (1)

2 Exactly when will he arrive?

.... (1)

SEG 1994

LISTENING E Weather forecasts are often used as material for Listening exercises. Here are two examples, the first requiring answers in English, the second requiring you to pick out the appropriate type of weather from a list.

1 You are on holiday in Normandy and hear the following weather forecast.

(a) What will the weather be early in the morning?

.... (1)

(b) What will the weather be later?

.... (1)

(c) What will the temperature be on the coast?

.... (1)

(d) Why will it only reach this temperature?

.... (1)

SEG 1993

2 You will hear a weather forecast from French radio. Look at the list A–F below.

Now listen to the forecast and, for each area mentioned in questions (a)–(e), pick out from the list the type of weather described and write the letter after the area. The areas are mentioned in the order of questions (a)–(e). You will not use all the letters.

A stormy
B rainy
C windy
D sunny
E cold
F foggy

(a) Bretagne .... (1)

(b) Normandie .... (1)

(c) Alsace Lorraine .... (1)

(d) Massif Central .... (1)

(e) Provence .... (1)

(5)

MEG 1994

You will sometimes be required to follow a plan or map while listening to instructions in French. In this example you have to show understanding of individual words and also follow the directions given round a house. Then you have to listen out for specific details about the garage and garden.

You will hear Sabine, a girl from a small village in Luxembourg, talking about her house. Look at the plan of the house and the questions below.

Now listen to Sabine describing her house and write the names of the rooms, in English, in the correct places on the plan (one room has been written in already). Then answer question 2. The X marks the place where you are at the start.

1 Write the names of the rooms, **in English**, in the correct places.

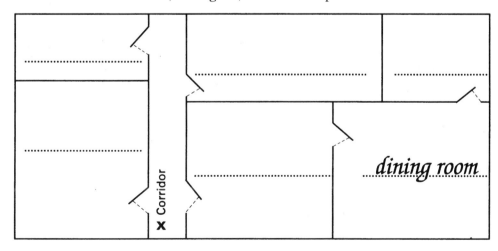

(5)

2 What does Sabine say about:

(a) the garage?

.... (1)

(b) the garden?

(i) .... (1)

(ii) .... (1)

(iii) .... (1)

(9)

MEG 1994

HIGHER

At this level, the pace of the French generally increases. There is a greater variety of voices and exercise type. The passages are generally longer and the vocabulary broader. A variety of tenses will be used.

Although you are still required to listen for specific details, you are also asked to understand the general gist of what is being said, to consider the mood or emotion of the speakers and to draw conclusions from what you hear.

You will generally find that you have to listen to both playings of the text. Don't worry if you don't understand the first time – make notes on what you understand and write your answers when you have listened again.

> As the Higher Level exercises are more difficult, each has been recorded twice on your cassette as is usually the case in the exam. The pauses between the playings, however, have been cut shorter. Stop the cassette at the end of the first playing for 20–30 seconds while you write any answers you want to at this stage. Then restart the cassette and listen again carefully, pause at the end for a further 20–30 seconds and write the remaining answers.

LISTENING G

In this opening example, the speaker uses past tenses to describe her early life. Pause the cassette as necessary to write your answers.

While on holiday in France, you attended a talk by Nicole Viloton, a young photographer who had just returned from an expedition in Australia.

1 Nicole talked about herself. Where was she born?

.... (1)

2 What does she say about where she lived? Mention **two** things.

....

.... (2)

3 What **two** ambitions did she have when she was a little girl?

....

.... (2)

4 When did she decide to become a photographer?

.... (1)

5 Nicole then went on to talk about her Australian expedition. How long did she take to cross Australia?

.... (1)

SEB 1994

In this next exercise the material is much denser and is presented in the form of a conversation. Notice that the questions do not simply ask you to pick out individual details but also to consider the speakers' emotions. You need to listen carefully twice.

LISTENING H

Questions **1–5**: Listen to this conversation between two teenage girls called Chantal and Annette, then answer **in English** the questions which follow.

1 What does Chantal want to do tomorrow?

.... (1)

2 Why won't Annette's boyfriend be able to come?

.... (1)

3 Why do you think Chantal is blushing?

....

.... (2)

4 How did Chantal spend yesterday evening?

....

.... (2)

5 What does Annette appear to think of her brother?

....

.... (1)

SEG 1993

LISTENING I

Here is an example of an exercise in which you listen for gist. Rather than picking out a specific detail, you need to listen to each extract and decide which alternative best matches its content.

You will hear five brief items from French radio. Look at the list **A–F** below. Now listen to the five items and, for each one, match its content with one of the descriptions in the list. Write the letter you choose from the list in the space after the question number. You will not use all the letters. You will hear the items in the order of questions **1–5**.

A forthcoming event	**1**	....	(1)
B advertisement	**2**	....	(1)
C sports report	**3**	....	(1)
D traffic report	**4**	....	(1)
E crime report	**5**	....	(1)
F weather report			(5)

MEG 1994

LISTENING J

Understanding problems and people's reactions to them will often be tested at Higher Level. Listen to this example making sure, as always, that you have taken time to read the questions carefully beforehand. You will notice that the French is spoken considerably more quickly now.

The context of this piece involves French parents taking English exchange partners to St. Malo to take the boat home.

1 You go to the ferry terminal in St. Malo with Sylvie's mother. At the ticket office the clerk explains there is a problem.

(i) What is the problem?

....

.... (2)

(ii) What solution does he offer?

.... (1)

2 Sylvie's mother then goes back to the desk to talk to the clerk.

(a) (i) How does she react?

.... (1)

(ii) Why does she feel like this?

.... (1)

(iii) How does the clerk respond?

.... (2)

(iv) What does Sylvie's mother finally decide to do?

.... (1)

(b) Then just before you leave, what do Sylvie's parents say to you?

....

....

.... (3)

NEAB 1994

The next example asks you both to pick out details (from information given in the present and the past tense) and to draw a conclusion about the speaker's feelings.

LISTENING K

One evening during your stay in France, your friend's neighbour, Jean-Paul, comes to visit. He tells you about his work.

1 When a client wants a house built, what is the first thing Jean-Paul does?

.... (1)

2 Apart from building houses, he mentions two other types of work he is often asked to do. Give **one** of them.

.... (1)

3 (a) What job was he asked to do last year?

.... (1)

(b) Why was this difficult?

....

.... (2)

4 Which word best expresses Jean-Paul's feelings about being asked to do this job? Put a tick beside the word you choose.

nervous ....   pleased ....   indifferent ....   worried .... (1)

ULEAC 1994

The subject matter in this next exercise is less familiar and therefore more difficult. A Russian pianist is talking (in French of course!) about why he left his native country, about his thoughts, his dreams and his regrets.

1   This is an interview with a famous Russian pianist who left Russia some years ago to play in the West.

(a) Why did he leave?

.... (1)

(b) What are his feelings about Russia today?

....

.... (2)

2   He visited Russia in 1989.

(a) Whom did he meet?

.... (1)

(b) What **two** things does he say about her?

....

.... (2)

3   (a) What is his dream?

.... (1)

(b) What does he regret about his life so far?

.... (1)

SEB 1994

Here is an exercise in which the only pauses included are natural ones as it is one side of a two-way telephone conversation. Your pen-friend's mother, Madame Cabillic, is on the phone to the doctor.

1   Why does Madame Cabillic apologise to the doctor?

.... (1)

2 Who is she phoning about?

.... (1)

3 What is the main problem? (Tick **one** only)

very high temperature ....   continuous vomiting ....

severe chest pains   ....   very bad coughing   .... (1)

4 What medicine is to be given?

.... (1)

5 When will the doctor be able to visit?

.... (1)

MEG 1994

Here is another example of an exercise in which you hear one half of a phone conversation. The conversation is between your pen-friend's mother and her husband who has called from work.
Listen carefully to both playings before answering the questions.

LISTENING N

1 Who is coming to dinner?

.... (2)

2 Give **two** reasons why your pen-friend's mother is annoyed.

....

.... (2)

3 How long has the foreigner been in France?

.... (1)

4 What effect does she hope that has had on him?

.... (1)

5 On what day will they be coming to dinner, and why was that day chosen?

.... (2)

SEG 1994

The skill in the next item involves drawing a conclusion about a situation. You also have to deal with a fairly strong accent used by the second speaker.

While driving in France during the summer holidays with your family the traffic suddenly comes to a standstill. After sitting in the car for a while you decide to find out what is happening. Two other drivers are discussing the situation. This is part of their conversation.

(a) Why is Driver A so upset?

....

.... (3)

(b) Who is causing the hold-up according to Driver B?

.... (1)

(c) What does he think these people should really be doing?

....

.... (3)

NICCEA 1994

Sometimes on Higher Level Listening exercises you have to deal with a fair amount of 'redundant material', i.e. text on which no questions are asked. The skill involved is to try to pick out the information required for answering the questions from fairly dense text. Furthermore, the subject matter used at this level can be fairly unfamiliar – that is, it is not an everyday situation such as those used at Basic Level.

This is the most difficult of the Listening exercises. Remember the hints: take time to read the questions and underline any key words (e.g. who; attitude; sad fact). Listen carefully to both playings and concentrate on general understanding during the first listening (perhaps taking a few notes) and write your answers during the pauses on the second listening. Check that what you have written makes sense and is legible, make any changes clear and, if you have left any question unanswered, make a sensible guess – you might be lucky, and you won't lose any marks if it's wrong. You have to be careful, however, not to add something incorrect to an otherwise correct answer – this will result in your losing the mark.

> N.B. For this final exercise the pauses during the playing have been included. You should pause the cassette for about 25 seconds between the two playings.

You will hear a radio report about some orphan children from Bangladesh (*des orphelins du Bengladesh*) who have just arrived at Charles de Gaulle airport near Paris. As well as hearing the reporter, you will also hear two women speaking.

1 In his opening comments, what does the reporter believe the smile on the children's faces represents? (Tick **one** only)

relief   ....   satisfaction   ....

happiness   ....   hope   ....   (1)

2 For how long had the children been waiting for this trip to France?

.... (1)

3 Who had come to meet them at the airport?

.... (1)

First woman speaker:

4 What is her attitude to the children?

.... (1)

5 What change in her family's eating habits does she predict?

.... (1)

Second woman speaker:

6 What evidence is there of her good nature?

.... (1)

7 What sad fact do we learn from the reporter's closing comments?

.... (1)

MEG 1994

3 Reading

REVISION HINTS

Many of the hints given for revising for the Listening exam apply equally well to Reading. Regular practice throughout the year leading up to the examination is the best revision method. But what is the best way of practising for the Reading exam?

Trying the exercises in this section along with any other sample exam materials you can find obviously provides you with good practice. Study the answers and the Examiner's tips carefully after you have tried the exercises, and make a note of where you went wrong. Note also any vocabulary which is new to you in the texts – it's surprising how often the same words can crop up from one exam to another, even though the texts will always be different.

You need to learn vocabulary on a regular basis. You may well have vocabulary lists, either in a text book, in a published French word list or in materials given to you by your teacher during the course. You may have managed to acquire the 'Defined Content' published by the Examination Board for which you are being prepared. This lists all the words that you can be tested on in the exam. But whatever materials you have, the secret is to try to learn a reasonable amount on a regular basis. In other words, set yourself targets at the start of the year of one page or one section per week, rather than attempting to learn long lists of words shortly before the exam. Establish a regular time of the week which you will devote to learning French vocabulary (and this of course will aid your revision for all the components). In this way, provided you plan well in advance, you need only aim to cover a small section each week. It's probably best to stick to one particular **topic** at a time.

But how do you learn vocabulary? Read through your chosen section several times, reading the words **aloud**. Then test yourself by seeing how many you can remember, by covering up the French and then the English. Ask a friend or relative to test you. Work together with friends preparing for the same exam. Put a mark next to those that you don't remember. It sometimes helps to copy down those words which you tend to forget so that you can concentrate on learning those – writing them down will help you remember them. However, it is always useful to try to **use** the words, in context, in speaking and writing. By using them in this way you will find that they 'stick' much more easily.

EXAMINATION HINTS

If you need to revise this subject more thoroughly, see the relevant topics in the *Letts* GCSE French Study Guide.

Again, the hints given in the Listening Revision summary apply to a large extent to examination technique in Reading. On both papers, answers are given in English, so you need to check at all times that you are answering the questions in a clear and legible way. Be sure that your answers make sense and provide the information required – re-read each question and answer after you have completed it.

Don't rush through the Basic Level paper. Even though you may find the questions easy, you should always take great care. At the same time, don't spend too long on any item which you find difficult. Come back to it later – but make a note that you have left it unanswered! If you are doing an exam in which the Higher follows the Basic in the same session, you may go on to the Higher paper or papers when you have finished the Basic, but don't forget that your first paper will be collected after 25 or 30 minutes and that you will obviously not be able to check it once it has been collected, so work through each paper carefully and thoroughly. See if you have time to check your work, but remember that the Higher papers need more time and care, so always keep an eye on the time.

Do check that you have not missed any answers. Many candidates each year turn two pages by mistake, or fail to turn over the final page. Examination papers always have each page numbered – so check!

READING QUESTIONS

The Basic or Foundation Level papers usually start by asking you to explain some common French signs or brief notices. You either know the words or not, but you can often get an idea of the likely meaning by reading and thinking carefully about the context presented in the question.
Here are some simple examples to start you off.

You are spending some time in Caen with your French pen-friend and his family.

1   Your friend asks you to come and meet him at school on your first day in Caen. You see this sign on the school gate.

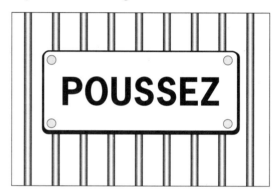

What does it say?

.... (1)

2   Next you notice this sign.

What do they sell here?

.... (1)

3   Nearby there is another sign.

What can you buy at 'Cléo'?

.... (1)

NEAB 1993

You may be required to take your pick from alternatives offered as in these next two examples:

1   You arrive at a skating rink in France. Which sign shows you the way in? (Tick one)

SORTIE ☐

OUVERT ☐

ENTRÉE ☐

PARKING ☐   (1)

2   In the supermarket you are looking for the meat counter. Which of the following signs do you look for? (Tick one)

Boulangerie ☐

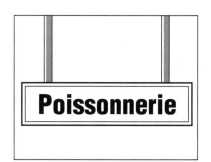
Poissonnerie ☐

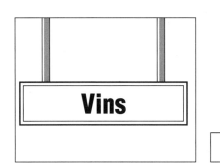
Vins ☐

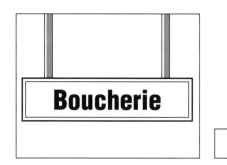
Boucherie ☐   (1)

MEG 1994

Letts
Q&A

Next, you are likely to be asked to pick out key words from a longer sequence. These next examples are still easy, but you need to search for the key words.

1 While shopping in France you buy a variety of soups.

What two vegetables does this soup contain?

....

.... (2)

2 Your family ate in this restaurant in Tours during your holiday in France. Your mother chose the speciality.

What did she eat?

.... (1)

3 You received this card from a French family you met on holiday.

Sophie et Emmanuel
sont heureux de vous annoncer la naissance de

Céline

Le 29 Octobre 1993
S et E Évrard

62, rue de Dunkerque 62500 ST OMER

What event is it announcing?

.... (1)

NICCEA 1994

Sometimes you can be asked a number of questions on a single, longer item such as an advertisement.

DESTOCKAGE MASSIF

pour changement d'enseigne

SUPER REMISES

sur tous nos articles

LA PLUS GRANDE SURFACE DE CUIR DE VOTRE RÉGION

HABILLEZ-VOUS EN CUIR POUR LE PRIX DU TEXTILE TOUT EN GARDANT LA QUALITÉ

SUPER DÉPOT

Route de Tulle (Entre Cuisines Plus et Tousalon)
MALEMORT - Tél. 55 92 11 78   FACILITES DE PAIEMENT

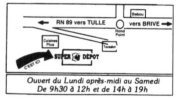
Ouvert du Lundi après-midi au Samedi
De 9h30 à 12h et de 14h à 19h

(a) What are the clothes in this shop made of?

.... (1)

(b) The shop claims to be number one for quality and advice. What two other things does it say it is best at?

(i) ....

(ii) .... (2)

(c) On which day of the week does the shop not open at all?

.... (1)

(d) At what time does it close in the evenings?

.... (1)

WJEC 1994

Information to study is sometimes presented in the form of a grid. Take care to study it carefully – it is so easy to make mistakes by working too quickly.

This is an advertisement for a hotel.

SEJOUR	CHAMBRES WC		DEMI-PENSION		PENSION COMPLETE	
PLUS DE 3 NUITS	BAINS	DOUCHE	BAINS	DOUCHE	BAINS	DOUCHE
HAUTE SAISON 1 personne 2 personnes	260 185	240 175	410 335	390 325	530 455	510 445
BASSE SAISON 1 personne 2 personnes	230 160	210 150	330 260	310 250	400 330	380 320

HAUTE SAISON:

juillet-août.

PETIT DEJEUNER:

30 francs par personne.

ANIMAL:

40 francs par jour (non admis au Restaurant).

CONDITIONS GENERALES

La chambre doit être libérée pour 12 heures.

Séjour gratuit pour un enfant de moins de 12 ans.

(a) How much will it cost you for half board for one person in a room with a shower in July?

.... (1)

(b) How much will you pay for a child of 11?

.... (1)

SEG 1993

You will always be tested on your ability to read and understand hand-written as well as printed French. Usually the writing will be reasonably easy to decipher, but it does differ from English hand-writing, so you need to practise reading it. In this example you will have no problems – but you have to scan through for the right information.

After you return home, you receive a note from a French friend who will soon be coming to stay with you in Scotland.

Aix, le 20 juillet

Merci de ta lettre. J'attends avec impatience ma visite en Écosse. J'arrive à l'aéroport d'Edimbourg mardi, 26 juillet à quatre heures de l'après-midi. Veux-tu bien venir me chercher?

Pendant mon séjour en Écosse, je voudrais faire des promenades à la montagne et voir le monstre célèbre du Loch Ness. Je voudrais aussi manger des spécialités écossaises—le saumon par exemple.

Qu'est-ce que tu voudrais comme cadeau de la France?

Amitiés,

Francine

(a) Where do you have to meet her? When?

....

....

.... (3)

(b) List three things she would like to do in Scotland.

....

....

.... (3)

This next passage of hand-writing, however, is much more challenging.

This is part of a letter from a French pen-friend telling you about his stay in a summer camp.

> ... Pendant les grandes vacances, j'ai passé une quinzaine dans une colonie de vacances située sur la côte sud de la Bretagne. On logeait dans de grandes tentes et il y avait toutes sortes d'activités. Je te raconte une journée typique.
>
> Le matin on se levait tôt, vers 7 heures. Après le petit déjeuner on devait aider à faire la vaisselle et à préparer le déjeuner – ça, je ne l'ai pas aimé, tu sais.
>
> Le matin on avait le choix de plusieurs activités. Pendant le séjour, j'ai appris à faire de la poterie, j'ai joué trois ou quatre fois au volley et j'ai fait de l'équitation pour la première fois.
>
> L'après-midi on est allé à la plage qui se trouvait à cinq cents mètres de la colonie où on a fait une promenade. Un jour on est allé faire des courses à Brest.

Read it and answer the questions below.

(a) How long did he spend there?

.... (1)

(b) Where exactly in Brittany was the summer camp?

....

.... (2)

(c) What happened at 7 a.m.?

.... (1)

(d) What did they do after breakfast?

....

....

.... (3)

(e) How often did he play volleyball?

.... (1)

(f) Name **two** other activities he took part in.

....

....

.... (2)

(g) How far away was the beach?

.... (1)

(h) What did they do in Brest?

.... (1)

SEG 1993

READING H And a final hand-written test where the style really is French and you have the added difficulty of scanning through a number of separate extracts to find the answers.

While you are in France you visit your friend Luc who is staying with his penpal, Paul. You see these messages on the pinboard in his room and ask him questions about them.

Ne fais pas de bruit – papa dort ! *Paul*	Rendez-vous avec Marc le lundi, 19 à 20h devant la gare routière ! OK ? *Paul*
Passe à la librairie (rue St. Jacques) chercher 'Paris Hit'. Je n'ai pas de monnaie – je t'en donnerai ce soir ! *Paul*	Télé en panne – M. Vallier passera la réparer ce matin – avant midi ! *Paul*
Ta mère a téléphoné – elle te rappellera ce soir assez tard ! *Paul*	Donne à manger au chien – petit bol dans le placard à droite de la machine à laver ! *Paul*

(a) Why were you asked not to make noise?

.... (1)

(b) Where were you to go for Paul's magazine 'Podium Hit'?

.... (1)

(c) When was your mother to ring you back?

.... (1)

(d) What were you to do at 20.00 hours on the evening of the 19th?

....

.... (2)

(e) Why was M. Vallier calling one morning?

.... (1)

(f) Where did you find the dog's bowl?

....

....

.... (3)

NICCEA 1992

HIGHER

The increase in difficulty from Basic to Higher Level in Reading is similar to that in Listening. Texts are longer and more dense, extra topic areas are covered and more complex vocabulary and structures are tested. In addition, you are required to pick out important points and themes and to identify gist rather than simply show understanding of single words or short phrases. And as in Listening, you have to identify attitudes, ideas and emotions and draw conclusions from what you read.

All this means that it is important to work slowly and carefully, to read texts thoroughly before answering the questions and to take care to write answers that are clear, unambiguous and complete.

READING I

Although texts tend to be much longer at the Higher Level, you can have brief items, but you will be required to understand more than simply single words. Here are two short examples.

You are in France with your penfriend.

1   On your first day you spend some time looking round the shops. You see this sign in a shop window.

APPRENEZ à CONDUIRE à PARTIR de 16 ans

What is it advertising?

....

.... (2)

2   In a department store you pick up this leaflet.

PORTRAIT RÉALISÉ
PAR
ORDINATEUR

What service is it offering?

.... (1)

NEAB 1994

In this next example, although still short, use is made of different tenses and you have to draw a conclusion on Question (d) on the basis of the material supplied.

Below you will see the horoscope for Libra (Balance).

23 sept. – 22 oct.

Vous avez dansé toute la nuit... Vous avez mangé la soupe à l'oignon, mais vous réussirez tout de même à faire un jogging matinal. Vous réussirez à profiter de ce premier jour de l'année sur tous les plans.

(a) Why might you be feeling tired this morning?

.... (2)

(b) What have you been eating?

.... (2)

(c) Why might you still be pleased with yourself this morning?

.... (1)

(d) On which day of the year do you think this horoscope appeared?

.... (1)

WJEC 1994

Here is another short text, but in this case you have to extract the gist of particular pieces of advice it contains.

You explain to your father what this leaflet says about driving at night.

**Attention
à la fatigue**

La fatigue provoque une diminu-tion des réflexes, voire le sommeil au volant. Avant de partir pour une longue route de nuit, reposez-vous quelques heures. Faites un repas léger. N'absorbez ni boisson alcoolisée ni médicament suscepti-ble de provoquer une somnolence.

Give **three** of the pieces of advice given to drivers before they undertake long night journeys.

....

....

.... (3)

NICCEA 1994

You mustn't be put off by difficult vocabulary. Higher Level texts will always contain certain words that you won't know. The test is to extract the meaning on the basis of understanding of those words which are familiar to you. Here is an example taken from a tourist leaflet.

While on holiday in the town of Carcassonne you want to visit the surrounding area called the AUDE. You are looking at a leaflet from the tourist office.

L'AUDE TOURISTIQUE

Découverte de l'Aude au départ de Carcassonne

L e département de l'Aude a pris le nom de la rivière qui le traverse. Sa superficie est de 634 435 hectares. Il compte 305 447 habitants. Il est situé au sud de la France, dans la partie occidentale du Languedoc-Roussillon, sa région administrative. L'agriculture occupe la première place dans les activités humaines en particulier à cause des vins qu'on produit. Par contre l'activité industrielle est peu importante. L'Aude est doué naturellement pour le tourisme: un climat généralement doux et sec, des paysages variés à l'infini (mer, montagne, collines boisées, gorges, garrigues) et une histoire culturelle exceptionnelle.

Nous vous proposons dans les pages suivantes la découverte des merveilles de notre département.

La situation géographique des régions ainsi que les distances sont calculées au départ de Carcassonne et pour faciliter l'organisation de votre circuit, nous vous indiquerons les cartes routières nécessaires.

Bon séjour à Carcassonne et dans l'Aude.

(a) How many people live in the Aude at present?

.... (1)

(b) What is the main working occupation of the people living in the Aude?

.... (1)

(c) What does the leaflet say about the local climate?

It is .... and .... (2)

(d) Apart from the climate what else adds to the tourist attraction of the area?

(i) ....

(ii) .... (2)

(e) How does the leaflet say that it will help tourists organise their visits to the area?

.... (1)

ULEAC 1994

Don't always expect the answers to come in the order that the information appears in the text, and be prepared to have to look more than once to find where the information is! That is certainly the case in this next example.

Whilst staying in France, you are looking to see what is on television and see this item in the newspaper. Read it carefully, then answer **in English** the questions which accompany it.

13.00	**JOURNAL**
13.35	MÉTÉO
13.40	**LES ENQUÊTES DU COMMISSAIRE MAIGRET**

MAIGRET EN ARIZONA 77
Adaptation de Jacques Rémy et Stéphane Bertin
Réalisation de Stéphane Bertin

Maigret	**Jean Richard**
L'inspecteur Lucas	**François Cadet**
L'agent Harry Cole	**Jess Hahn**
Le shérif O'Rourke	**William Lang**
Bessy Mitchell	**Babette Propps**

Diffusé en 1986, 1988, 1989, 1990

LE SUJET
A Tucson, dans l'Arizona. En assistant au déroulement d'une enquête criminelle, le commissaire Maigret découvre la vie, les mœurs, et les structures policières et judiciaires de cette ville de l'Ouest américain.

SI VOUS AVEZ MANQUÉ LE DÉBUT
Le commissaire Maigret et l'inspecteur Lucas sont en voyage d'information aux États-Unis depuis trois semaines. Ils arrivent à l'aéroport de Dallas (Texas) où ils doivent retrouver un agent du FBI, Harry Cole, qui n'est pas au rendez-vous. Il a laissé un message demandant à Maigret de venir le rejoindre à Tucson où une affaire de drogue le retient...

(a) How many times has this film been broadcast previously?

.... (1)

(b) How do Maigret and his assistant travel to Dallas?

.... (1)

(c) In what way do they have to change their plans when they arrive in Dallas, and why?

....

.... (2)

(d) How do they know where to go?

.... (1)

(e) If you switched on five minutes early, what would you see?

.... (1)

SEG 1993

You are sometimes asked to match up brief summaries of items with the appropriate extracts. Try this next item – but don't forget to read the instructions!

Answer the questions by putting the appropriate letter in the boxes provided. You may not need all the letters. You may need some letters more than once.

BALANCE
(23 septembre - 22 octobre)
Un mois qui s'annonce bien et qui vous donne envie d'oublier vite les soucis passés.

VIERGE
(23 août - 22 septembre)
Vous n'aurez pas d'efforts à faire pour être joyeux et détendu. La vie vous sourit. Vous aurez un amour d'été qui pourrait durer.

CAPRICORNE

(21 décembre - 19 janvier)

Vous retrouvez votre optimisme. L'amour arrivera dans votre vie. Tout se passera très bien jusqu'à la fin du mois quand une dispute vous séparera.

 POISSONS

(19 février - 20 mars)

Un mois superbe s'annonce. Vous voulez passer de bonnes vacances et vous réussirez.

 TAUREAU

(21 avril - 20 mai)

Vous allez passer un mois dans une ambiance joyeuse. Vacances très réussies.

 BÉLIER

(21 mars - 20 avril)

Un mois assez agréable. Même si tout n'est pas parfait vous êtes décidé à prendre la vie du bon côté.

 SCORPION

(23 octobre - 21 novembre)

Vous aurez beaucoup d'amis autour de vous. Vous aurez des journées bien remplies et vous ne vous ennuierez pas un seul instant.

 VERSEAU

(20 janvier - 18 février)

Vous vous ouvrez à de nouveaux intérêts et vous faites de nouveaux amis. La deuxième partie du mois sera plus agréable.

Which horoscope most clearly predicts that the person born under that sign will:

1 …be surrounded by friends and will certainly not be bored?

2 …have a summer holiday romance that could continue after the holidays?

3 …have a summer holiday romance that will end in an argument?

4 …have a better second half of the month?

5 …forget his/her worries?

6 …find it easy to relax?

(6)

MEG 1994

In the most difficult reading comprehension exercises, the questions often seem to become less structured and ask you to extract what you consider to be the most important points from a text or, as in the listening, to draw a conclusion. Here are two examples to illustrate these points.

While having a drink in a café you look at a newspaper you have just bought and notice this advertisement.

READING O

**Le dimanche si vous préférez le cinéma
vous êtes libre d'aller au cinéma,
mais si vous préférez vous acheter
un bon livre ou un bon disque
vous êtes libre d'aller au cinéma.**

La loi autorise l'ouverture des cinémas, des musées et des théâtres
le dimanche – elle ne doit pas interdire celle des librairies et des
magasins de disques –

Virgin MEGASTORE
BORDEAUX. 15-19, place Gambetta. PARIS. 52-60, avenue des Champs-Élysées.
MARSEILLE. 75, rue St-Ferréol.

What is the point of the advertisement?

....

.... (2)

NEAB 1993

On a newspaper page, you see this report.

READING P

Pagaille dans la rue

Mardi, les infirmières ont manifesté pour la cinquième fois depuis septembre. Les médecins et l'ensemble des travailleurs des hôpitaux ont suivi le mouvement. Il faut dire que tout le monde est très choqué depuis la manifestation du 17 octobre. Ce jour-là, les infirmières qui voulaient aller à l'Elysée (là où travaille le président de la République) ont été reçues par des gaz lacrymogènes (gaz qui font pleurer) et un canon à eau (de l'eau envoyée avec beaucoup de puissance pour faire reculer les gens). Deux infirmières ont été blessées. Cela a révolté beaucoup de Français parce que les infirmières ne sont pas violentes. Elles continueront à manifester tant qu'elles ne seront pas mieux payées (une infirmière gagne 7100 F net par mois. Net, c'est ce qu'on a vraiment comme argent pour vivre).

Give **four** of what you consider to be the most important points made here.

....

....

....

....

....

.... (4)

NEAB 1993

This exercise again requires very thorough reading of the text and careful study of the questions before answering. It is a good example of the way in which Higher Level exercises often test your understanding of the emotions and attitudes expressed.

In the magazine *Jeune et Jolie* you come across the 'courrier du coeur'. Read this letter from a reader and the answer to it.

CHERE Julie

Vague à l'âme? Blues au coeur?
Vous vous sentez seule et abandonnée?
Plus maintenant!
Jeune et Jolie est là pour répondre à vos problèmes.
Écrivez à Jeune et Jolie, 63 Champs-Élysées, 75008 Paris.

Chère Julie,
Je t'écris parce que j'ai un gros problème. Je m'appelle Sandra et j'ai quinze ans. Je suis déjà sortie avec plusieurs garçons. Un jour ma soeur m'a présentée à Fabrice. Il est drôle et très gentil et on m'a dit qu'il est très sensible, mais il n'est pas beau. Autant dire que s'il n'avait pas de beaux yeux il serait carrément horrible. Ma soeur m'a dit qu'il était très amoureux de moi et qu'il voudrait sortir avec moi. Quand j'ai parlé avec ma meilleure copine, elle s'est moquée de moi, elle a ri, et elle m'a conseillé de laisser tomber. Je suis vraiment désespérée car il est si gentil et sensible que j'ai peur de le blesser en lui disant non.
Aide-moi.
Sandra

La réponse de Julie.
Il serait préférable que tu prennes tes décisions toi-même et que tu ne te laisses pas dicter ta conduite et tes actes par ta meilleure amie. En effet, qui est plus capable que toi de choisir la suite que tu dois donner ou pas à cette histoire? Tu as su découvrir chez ce garçon ce qu'il y a de bien plus important que l'apparence physique, la gentillesse. Evidemment, à ton âge, on est bien plus attiré par le côté visible des choses. On a envie de montrer à ses copines que l'on a trouvé le plus beau. Mais ce n'est pas suffisant pour faire une histoire d'amour forte et durable. Réfléchis bien avant de briser un coeur et décide toute seule de ce que tu dois faire. Surtout ne sors pas avec lui parce que tu n'oses pas lui dire non: ce serait pire pour lui et pour toi. Il ne faut jamais forcer ses sentiments, ni dans un sens, ni dans l'autre.

Answer these questions **in English**.

1 What does Sandra know about Fabrice's character and personality?

(i) .... (1)

(ii) .... (1)

(iii) .... (1)

2 What was the reaction of Sandra's best friend and what was her advice, when Sandra spoke to her?

(i) Reaction .... (1)

(ii) Advice .... (1)

3 Why is Sandra worried about rejecting Fabrice?

.... (1)

4 According to Julie, what shows that girls of Sandra's age find physical appearance important?

.... (1)

5 According to Julie, what would be the worst outcome of this situation for both Sandra and Fabrice?

.... (1)

(8)

MEG 1994

Here are two Higher Level exercises with a hand-written text.

Although in this first example the writing is not difficult to decipher, the text is very dense and again the questions are general, requiring understanding of more than simple individual details. You need to read the whole text carefully before you decide on your answers and you should bear in mind the mark allocations.

READING R

A French Canadian visitor comes to your school and you ask him to write something about French-speaking Canada for you. This is what he writes.

Bonjour à tous.

Je m'appelle Frédéric Dompierre, j'ai vingt-six ans et je viens du Canada. Au Canada il y a une province appelée le Québec et dans cette province, près de six millions de personnes parlent français. Je suis donc québécois ou canadien-français, c'est la même chose.

La ville où j'habite s'appelle Montréal. C'est une ville de deux millions d'habitants. L'hiver au Canada est très froid. Au mois de janvier la température descend parfois jusqu'à trente-cinq degrés sous zéro. Il y a également de grosses chutes de neige. Jusqu'à 1 mètre, 1 mètre 50. Même deux mètres dans les régions plus au nord.

À Montréal, j'habite avec ma femme qui s'appelle Lucie. Elle n'est malheureusement pas venue en Angleterre. Elle viendra cependant me visiter à Noël.
J'ai deux soeurs et un frère. Ma première soeur s'appelle Violaine. Mon père s'est remarié avec une autre femme avec qui il a eu Jeanne et Philippe.
Ma mère s'appelle Ginette et elle est professeur. Mon père s'appelle François et il est compositeur (!).

Je suis venu en Angleterre comme assistant enseignant et je vais aider des étudiants en difficulté à apprendre le français.

Je vous dis au revoir et à bientôt.

Frédéric.

45

(a) What does he say about Quebec Province?

....

.... (1)

(b) What information does he give about the Canadian winter?

....

.... (2)

(c) What does he say about Lucie?

....

....

.... (3)

(d) Who are Jeanne and Philippe?

....

....

.... (2)

NEAB 1993

The writing is not as easy in this exercise, and the question is very general!

Your neighbours ask you to help them with this letter they have received from a French camp site.

CAMPING "LES ROCHES"
CAROUAL - VILLAGE
22430 ERQUY · Tél. 96 72 32 90
EURL au Capital de 50.000 F.
Siret 353 786 452 00014

Le 18/6

Madame, Monsieur,

Nous avons bien reçu votre chèque de 155,00F et vous en remercions.

Nous vous confirmons donc votre réservation d'un emplacement du 8 au 16 Août prochain.

A bientôt!

[signature] Barbedienne

What does the letter say?

....

....

.... (2)

NEAB 1993

47

This final Reading exercise presents a dense and fairly difficult text. It no doubt contains words that you do not know, but this should not prevent you from being able to answer the questions, provided you read the text very carefully to start with, and study the questions with equal care.

Read this article which recently appeared in a French magazine, then answer **in English** the questions which follow.

Les abandons: une vie de chien

Maîtres en vacances animaux en souffrance

Qu'y a-t-il dans le coeur de ces personnes qui traitent leurs amis à quatre pattes comme des «chiens», pour employer une expression courante, allant même jusqu'à les abandonner sur la route des vacances, parce qu'ils sont devenus trop encombrants?

Que faire de ces chiens et chats errants, souvent malades, que les pompiers prennent en charge tous les jours? Depuis le début de l'été les refuges affichent «complet»!

M. Jean-Luc Bordier, responsable du refuge Jean-Duflos, connaît bien le problème: «L'abandon de l'été est un phénomène malheureusement classique. En effet, ce sont souvent des chiens de six mois, nés en février, arrivant à maturité et trop bruyants et trop énergiques, qui deviennent gênants pour les vacances.»

On abandonne aussi des petits chats car il est plus facile de les laisser en liberté que de les tuer à la naissance. «Les jeunes gens abandonnent beaucoup leurs animaux, explique Jean-Luc Bordier, car ils changent souvent de domicile et ils ne peuvent plus en assurer la garde.»

Alors que faire? Les solutions ne sont pas nombreuses. Il y en a pourtant une, mais qui coûte un peu cher: la pension dans un chenil ou un refuge — une sorte d'hôtel pour les chiens — mais ces établissements sont plutôt rares en France. On devrait sûrement suivre l'exemple de nos cousins anglo-saxons, parce que dans chaque ville d'Angleterre on trouve plusieurs établissements de la sorte.

Un autre problème, c'est que de nombreux touristes perdent leurs chiens ou leurs chats et repartent chez eux. Si seulement ils avaient pensé à faire tatouer leur animal... Lorsqu'un animal est tatoué, il n'y a pas de problème pour retrouver les propriétaires qui sont souvent heureux de savoir que leur compagnon a été retrouvé.

(a) What attitude seems to lie behind the writer's opening remark?

.... (1)

(b) What behaviour is he talking about?

....

.... (2)

(c) Who first takes in the strays that are found every day?

.... (1)

(d) What dogs does Monsieur Bordier say are often involved?

....

.... (2)

(e) Why do their owners consider these dogs to be a nuisance?

....

.... (2)

(f) Why are little cats also abandoned?

....

.... (2)

(g) Why are young people often to blame?

....

.... (2)

(h) In what way are the English held up as a good example to the French?

.... (1)

(i) What sometimes happens when owners take their pets on holiday with them?

....

.... (2)

SEG 1993

REVISION HINTS

Writing is probably the most difficult of the skill areas in French but, as with the other skills, regular careful revision and practice provide the key to success. The same hints regarding the learning of vocabulary mentioned in the Reading section apply to Writing. At the same time, you need to revise the basic points of French grammar regularly. You may have a text book that provides a grammar summary at the back. Use it, but don't attempt to do too much at a time and remember to ask your teacher about anything that is not clear.

Pay particular attention to verbs – especially the irregular ones. You don't need to learn every part of every verb in the book – you wouldn't need them all and you probably wouldn't be able to learn them all. Concentrate on the first and third persons of the verb in the singular (*je* and *il/elle*) and in the plural (*nous* and *ils/elles*). Concentrate on the present tense, the perfect tense and the future tense (remembering that you can form a future tense by using the verb *aller* (to go) followed by the infinitive of the verb required (e.g. *je vais partir* – 'I'm going to leave'). Remember that you will also need to be able to form and use properly the imperfect tense at Higher Level.

Practise the exercises in this book and read the accompanying tips. Remember too what was said in the general hints – the more you practise **speaking** French the easier you will find the other skills. Similarly, reading French will help your writing skills.

EXAMINATION HINTS

On the Basic Level papers, the important thing is to convey the message. Spelling has to be accurate enough to be understood by a French person, but you will not lose too many marks for spelling errors. Check, then, that you have made the message clear, and that you have conveyed all the information required. You may be able to get round an idea even if you do not know a particular word – for example *sept jours* is a perfectly clear rendering of 'a week' if you have forgotten the word *une semaine*.

On the Higher Level papers, accuracy is much more important. Obviously you need to convey the message, and again you must be sure to include all the details asked for (tick them off on the paper as you do them) but then you must check for accuracy. If writing the past tense, have you included the part of *avoir* or *être* and have you included the right accent where it is required (e.g. *j'ai mangé*)? If you have written a plural, have you added the *s* to the noun and any adjective with it (e.g. *j'ai deux petits chiens*)? Re-read your work and look for errors and again, always ask yourself 'Is my writing clear enough to be read by the Examiner and have I made any changes clear?' Try to recall the sort of errors you have made previously when writing French and see if you can spot them. Apart from accents and plural endings mentioned above, try to avoid those common spelling errors that so many candidates make with such words as *beaucoup de/d'*; *mercredi*; *le petit déjeuner*; *soeur*; *vacances* (always plural) etc., and remember the difference between *chevaux* and *cheveux*, *vieille* and *la veille*, *mois* and *moins* and so on.

One final point: it is probably **not** a good idea to write a rough version of a French essay or letter first (you could well run out of time writing up the neat copy) but you should **write on every second line** to leave room for any changes you might make when checking.

If you need to revise this subject more thoroughly, see the relevant topics in the *Letts* GCSE *French Study Guide*.

This section of the book is in two parts. In the first part you will see some sample examination questions with suggested answers. In the second part, which starts on page 60, you will find more sample exam questions for you to try. There are no sample answers given to these, but you will find some hints as to how you might tackle the questions.

PART 1: SAMPLE QUESTIONS AND ANSWERS

The early exercises at Basic or Elementary Level usually consist of short lists of related words or brief notes or messages to be written in French. Here is a simple example of a 'lists' question.

You are in France at your pen-friend's house and you and your friend decide to go out on your bikes for a picnic the next day. Your pen-friend's mother is going shopping. Write her a list **in French** of 10 items of food to buy for the picnic (e.g. bread, ham, apples). Do **not** include drink, as you will take water bottles on the bikes. (10)

MEG 1994

BASIC

WRITING A

ANSWER

1. pain
2. croissants
3. tarte aux pommes
4. jambon
5. saucisson
6. pommes
7. poires
8. bananes
9. chocolat
10. chips

Examiner's commentary Spelling does not need to be perfect, but should be good enough to be understood by a French person. Try to avoid words which are exactly the same in French as in English such as *oranges*. Use the examples given in the instructions and they should remind you of related words (bakery items, fruits, meats etc.). Don't forget that *chips* mean 'crisps' in French.

WRITING B

You will usually need to write more than single words, of course. In this next example you have to come up with some simple phrases describing activities.

Your French exchange partner is visiting your area in July and you send this form to your pen-friend. Fill in each day with something interesting to do. Each day must be a different activity from the others. The first day has been done for you. Please complete the form in French. (8)

WJEC 1994

ANSWER

lundi	–	aller en ville
mardi	–	jouer au tennis
mercredi	–	visiter les amis
jeudi	–	nager a* la piscine
vendredi	–	voir un film au cinema*
samedi	–	acheter des souvenirs

Examiner's commentary Follow the pattern of the example given and try to find a different verb for each activity. Try not to repeat *aller* or *jouer* each time. *Did you spot the two missing accents (à, cinéma)? It's not too serious at this level, but you should try to remember them.

WRITING C

Writing or answering messages is a commonly set Writing task at this level. Sometimes they can be quite brief as this example.

Imagine that a French girl is staying at your house. One day, when she is out, her mother telephones. You write down the message for her in French, saying:

> who has telephoned
> that it is her grandfather's birthday next week
> and asking whether she has sent him a card. (6)

SEG 1993

ANSWER

Nicole! Ta mère a téléphoné à trois heures. C'est l'anniversaire de ton grand-père la semaine prochaine. Tu as envoyé une carte?

Examiner's commentary Now you need to use past tenses. It's a good idea to make up a name for the French friend. Notice too how adding a time makes the message more interesting. If you forgot the phrase *la semaine prochaine*, you could say *lundi prochain*, or, if you had forgotten *prochain*, you could make up a date like *lundi le quinze avril* and date the message *le dix avril*. You would really need to know the verb *envoyer*. Make sure you know it!

WRITING D

Message writing exercises usually include five or six tasks. Here is an example where you note the details of a 'phone call.

During your French friend's visit to your house his/her mother 'phones while he/she is out. Using the memo slip you write down the message for your friend **in French**. You should use 25–30 words and deal with all five points. Remember full sentences are not required.

1 The family is well.
2 Your brother is going to Germany on Friday.
3 Weather is very warm in France.
4 Your mother wants a postcard from Northern Ireland.
5 Give the day and date you are coming home. (20)

NICCEA 1992

La famille va bien. Ton frère va en Allemagne vendredi. Il fait très

chaud en France. Ta mère voudrait une carte postale de l'Irlande

du Nord. Quel jour et quelle date tu retourne* à la maison?

Examiner's commentary   Remember that you must use the verb *aller* when saying how you feel (hence *la famille va bien*) and always *je vais bien* for 'I am well'). To say 'on' a day, simply write the day, with no word before it. Note that in the last task the question is being asked to the French friend, so it would not be appropriate for you, as the message-taker, to provide the details. *There is one verb error here – try to remember that any verb in the *tu* form in the present tense (other than *tu peux* and *tu veux*) ends with the letter *s*. There would be no penalty here for failing to keep below 30 words.

You can also be expected to have to write postcards to a French pen-friend. Here is an example.

At the end of your holiday, you send your French friend a postcard and you invite him to visit you in Scotland.

Say when he can come to Scotland.

Write **three** sentences about where you live.   (10)

SEB 1994

Cher Pierre,

Tu veux venir me voir en Ecosse? Si tu veux, tu peux venir au mois de juillet. J'habite dans un petit village au bord de la mer.

Il y a une boulangerie, une épicerie et une poste. Dans mon village il y a environ mille habitants.

Amitiés,

Ton amie,

Anne.

Pierre Bordes

532, Rue d'Arras

59500

DOUAI

Examiner's commentary   To make it authentic, a name should be included for the pen-friend and the card should be signed. All tasks should be carried out. Notice how effectively the following simple but important phrases have been used: *tu veux* – 'you want', and *tu peux* – 'you can' (these phrases can be used as statements or, by simply adding a question mark, as questions); *il y a* – 'there is' or 'there are' (and again 'is there?' or 'are there?' by adding the question mark).

WRITING F

In some cases you are asked to write a reply to a message left for you in French. Note how use has been made in the answer below of phrases given in the stimulus message.

A French friend is staying in your home for a few days. You arrive home at midday to find that your guest has gone out and left a message for you. Since you have to go back to school in the afternoon you leave a reply to your friend's message. Your reply message is to be written **in French** and must contain the details set out below the first message.

> Tu n'étais pas là ce matin –
> tu as dû sortir de bonne heure !
> Après le petit déjeuner j'ai
> écrit des lettres à des copains.
> Il y a une boîte aux lettres
> près d'ici?
> Tu auras des devoirs de français
> à faire ce soir?
>
> A tout à l'heure
>
> C.

1 Thank your friend for the message.
2 Say that you left home at half past seven.
3 Ask if your friend also wrote to his/her parents.
4 Tell your friend there is a letterbox opposite the church.
5 Ask if your friend can help you with your French homework.

(10)

ULEAC 1994

ANSWER

Chère Catherine,

Je te remercie bien de ton message. J'ai dû sortir à sept heures et demi* ce matin. Tu as écrit des lettres à tes parents aussi? Il y a une boîte aux lettres en face de l'église. Tu peux m'aider avec mes devoirs de Français ce soir? Merci.

A tout à l'heure.

S.

Examiner's commentary   See again how questions can be written simply by writing the statement followed by the question mark. In this answer, much of the material in the first message has been used to good effect, including the ending. *The only error is in the spelling of *demi* which should have an *e* on the end (the only times for which the spelling *demi* is used for 'half past' are *midi* and *minuit* as they are both masculine).

When writing letters at Higher Level you usually have to write 100 or so words, though the number of words isn't as important as making sure that all the tasks have been done. Letters can be either informal (typically, to a French pen-friend) or formal (such as booking a room in a hotel, applying for a job etc.). You must learn the separate methods of starting and finishing letters of each type. Remember also that the *vous* form of address will always be used in formal letters whereas, in writing to a pen-friend, the *tu* form will be more appropriate. If writing to the pen-friend's family, however, you would have to use *vous* as you are addressing more than one person.

Here is an example of an informal letter.

You are planning to spend a week-end in Paris, travelling by air and staying in a hotel near the Louvre. A French friend has written to you saying she hopes you will be able to meet during the course of the week-end, and asking for details of your programme. Write a letter to her including the following points:

1   how you are travelling
2   where and at what time you arrive in and leave Paris
3   where you are staying
4   how you hope to spend the week-end (mention **two** activities)
5   suggesting you go out for a meal together on Saturday night
6   asking her to ring you at your hotel

Do not write more than about 100 words.

(60)

SEG 1993

Manchester   le 24 juillet

Chère Chantal,

Merci bien de ta lettre que j'ai reçue hier. Elle m'a fait grand plaisir.

Je vais prendre l'avion pour voyager à Paris. J'arriverai à l'aéroport Charles de Gaulle samedi matin, le cinq août à dix heures et quart. Je quitterai Paris dimanche soir, le six, à huit heures.

J'ai réservé une chambre à l'Hôtel Florence, près du Louvre. Pendant le weekend je voudrais visiter le Louvre et monter à la Tour Eiffel. Veux-tu dîner avec moi samedi soir? Si c'est possible, veux-tu me téléphoner à mon hôtel samedi vers six heures?

J'espère bien te voir pendant le weekend.

Amitiés,

Robert.

Examiner's commentary   It's important to read the instruction and each task carefully to be sure not to miss anything – don't forget that most marks are allocated to communicating the tasks, so it's obviously vital not to miss any or to overlook, for example, the 'double' tasks (**2** and **4**). Learn a standard introduction and ending to a letter of this type. The ones used above are good examples. Note how both methods of expressing the future tense have been used for talking about future plans. It's best not to use the verb *rester* for staying in a hotel – note how the idea has been expressed above. Otherwise, use *loger*.
This is a well-written letter that would gain an excellent mark. It impresses because the verbs are accurate. Notice too how well the separate ideas are connected through the use of words such as *pendant* and *pour*. Notice also how *veux-tu* has been used effectively in order to convey the idea of 'would you?' as well as 'would you like to?'.

55

WRITING H | Notice the important differences of style needed in the example of a formal letter which follows.

On the last day of your holiday in Ajaccio, Corsica, you lost your bag and its contents. You reported this at the police station but when you returned to Britain, you received a letter asking you to complete a full report in **French**.

1 Explain why you were in Ajaccio and where you were staying.
2 Describe what you lost. (Give **three** details.)
3 Say when you noticed your loss.
4 Say where you think you lost your bag.
5 Describe what you did about it.
6 Explain what problems the loss caused you.

(12)
NEAB 1993

ANSWER

REPUBLIQUE FRANÇAISE

MAIRIE D'AJACCIO
20000 AJACCIO

POLICE MUNICIPALE

Service des Épaves
☎ 95-21.90.15 (Poste 386)

Déclaration de Perte

Lichfield, le 2 septembre 1995

Monsieur/Madame,

Je vous écris pour vous donner des détails du sac que j'ai perdu pendant que j'étais en vacances à Ajaccio le mois dernier. J'étais en vacances avec ma famille et nous logions à l'Hôtel du Port.

J'ai perdu un sac en cuir rouge. Dans le sac il y avait des lunettes de soleil, mon portefeuille avec environ 500 francs dedans et mon passeport. J'ai perdu le sac samedi le 26 août vers deux heures de l'après-midi. Je pense que j'ai laissé le sac dans un magasin près du port. Je suis allée aux magasins pour le chercher, mais sans succès. Je suis allée aussi au poste de police pour donner des détails, comme vous savez.

J'ai eu beaucoup de problèmes à revenir en Angleterre sans mon passeport – j'ai dû attendre trois heures à la douane et je n'avais pas beaucoup d'argent.

J'espère que vous trouverez mon sac.

Je vous prie d'agréer, monsieur/madame, l'expression de mes sentiments distingués.

Mlle. Elizabeth Smith.

Examiner's commentary   Learn how to start and end letters of this type. Note the use of the imperfect tense to say where you were staying. This letter would gain a good mark because all the tasks are communicated clearly and accurately and there is a good range of verbs in the past tense with good constructions such as: *pendant que* + imperfect tense; *pour* + infinitive; *j'ai dû* + infinitive; *j'espère que* + future tense etc.

Note that, as this letter was written by a girl, she has to write *je suis allée* but remember that she does **not** need to add this extra *e* for verbs taking *avoir* in the perfect tense (e.g. *j'ai perdu*). Remember also the constructions *je pense que…* and *j'espère que…* . It is worth taking a little time to study this sample answer. There is some good writing on a commonly set subject for formal letters in examinations.

There are no errors in this letter, although it would have been better to write *comme vous le savez* for 'as you know'.

Advanced writing tasks will often provide the outline of a story in the form of a series of pictures. Here you are free to tell the story in your own words, although usually you are to assume that the events took place in the past, so you are obliged to use the past tenses. Note how the writer manages to set the scene, recount the events and make a suitable conclusion.

Imagine that the events in the pictures happened to you. Write an account **in French** of 100–120 words about the incident to a French friend.

(i)

(ii)

(iii)

(iv)

(80)

WJEC 1993

ANSWER

L'année dernière je suis allé en vacances en Bretagne avec ma soeur, Anne. Nous avons fait du camping. Le premier jour au camping il faisait très beau, donc nous avons décidé d'aller à la plage qui était à trois kilomètres de notre tente.

Nous nous sommes levés tôt et, après avoir pris le petit déjeuner, nous sommes partis à vélo. Nous avons pris nos raquettes de tennis avec nous.

A neuf heures, nous sommes arrivés à la plage. C'était très beau. Il y avait quelques personnes sur la plage – un homme lisait un journal et deux personnes se baignaient au soleil. La plage était très belle.

– Viens jouer sur la plage! a dit Anne.

Nous avons joué pendant une heure. Mais quand nous avons quitté la plage – désastre! Nos vélos n'étaient pas là et nos affaires non plus! Nous étions très fâchés. Et puis il a commencé à pleuvoir. Donc nous sommes rentrés au camping, tristes et mouillés. Et quand nous sommes arrivés au camping, nous avons trouvé que la tente est tombée*. Oh là là! Quelle journée!

Examiner's commentary The essay is a little too long, but the standard of French is very good. The writer has obviously learned how to use the perfect tense and knows the rules of agreement (e.g. *nous sommes arrivés*, *la plage était **belle*** etc.). All stages of the story have been well covered. Notice how effective it is to include some speech (but note also how you need to turn round the phrase 'she said' after speech – *a dit Anne*). *The only mistake is in *la tente **est** tombée* – it would be better to use the phrase for '**had** fallen' which would be ***était** tombée*.

Again, it is worth taking the time to study this good piece of writing and learn some of the effective phrases and constructions it contains. Note, for example:
- the imperfect tense to describe what the weather **was** like and what the people **were** doing on the beach.
- *à trois kilomètres* – expressions of distance require *à*.
- *décider + de +* the infinitive of the verb.
- reflexive verbs in the perfect tense, e.g. *nous nous sommes levés*.
- *pendant une heure* – **for** a period of time in the past tense.
- *commencer + à +* the infinitive of the verb.
- *après + avoir +* the past participle.
- the use of *donc* (or *alors*) meaning 'so' (i.e. 'therefore').

WRITING J The most difficult writing tasks may not necessarily require use of past tenses. In order to reach top grades you need to be able to give and justify opinions about certain issues or express feelings and emotions (we saw the same requirements in the Reading and Listening papers). Here is an example.

Your pen-friend has asked you to write an article for his/her school magazine on why you prefer living in town to living in the country or vice-versa. You should explain the advantages and disadvantages that make you prefer one to the other, giving as many reasons as you can to make sure you write the full 150 words. Write **in French**. (20)

MEG 1994

La campagne, c'est très beau! Je prefere* la campagne à la ville. La ville est moche! Quand on va à la campagne, de la ville, on va dans une autre monde*. Quelle différence!

Dans la campagne il n'y a personne près de vous. J'adore la campagne parce qu'il y a beaucoup de chose* à faire. Pendant l'été on peut faire un tour à vélo pour voir tout* les choses intéressantes. Aussi*, si on veut voir les collines, on peut y faire une promenade. Il y a beaucoup de rivières où on peut nager. J'aime faire du camping avec mes amis dans le forêt* et quelquefois nous prenons un pique-nique.

Malheureusement, c'est souvent ennuyeux à la campagne. Dans la ville il y a des discothèques, des bibliothèques, des magasins et le stade. C'est difficile d'aller là si vous habite* dans la campagne. Vous ne pouvez pas y aller à pied parce que c'est trop loin.

Mais malgré ces problèmes je prefere* les arbres, les animaux et les collines aux immeubles, aux voitures et aux foules de gens dans la ville!

Examiner's commentary   Although there are a few errors in this piece, the candidate has kept to the subject, has managed to give good and bad points about the town and country and has written a nice conclusion to the essay. The French is not particularly stylistic, but it is simple, clear and generally correct. For these reasons, the candidate would receive a good mark for this attempt.

It is sound advice in such writing tasks to keep to French that you are quite confident is correct, to keep to the subject and, obviously, to check very carefully afterwards for any errors.

*Errors in the above include: accents on *préfère*; **un** *monde*; *beaucoup de choses*; *toutes les choses*; *Aussi* should not be placed at the start of a sentence; *la* *forêt*, and *vous habitez*.

Note that it is possible to use either *dans la campagne* or *à la campagne*, but that *à* is more common. In the same way, *à* should be used to render 'at', 'in' or 'to' a named town, although you might sometimes see *dans Paris* meaning 'in the heart of Paris'. Note also how the writer, in giving the idea of what can be done in the country, correctly uses the word *on*, which is so much more common in French than is the word 'one' in English phrases such as 'one can'. Remember, though, that the good phrase *on peut* must be followed immediately by a verb in the **infinitive** (e.g. *on peut nager* or *on peut faire un tour*).

To prepare for essays of this type, which generally ask you to express your opinion, make sure you learn suitable phrases such as:

A mon avis – in my opinion.

Je pense que... – I think that..., in addition to the following which all have roughly the same meaning:

Je trouve que...; *je considère que...*; *j'ai l'impression que...*; *je crois que...*; *je dirais que...*

PART 2: PRACTICE QUESTIONS

BASIC

Here are some writing exercises for you to practise. They match fairly closely the style of questions you have seen in Part 1.

WRITING K

Your school has received exchange forms from a French school. Part of a form is shown below.

Fill in the section on interests with your **five** favourite hobbies (e.g. cars, stamps, reading, dancing). Do **not** include games or sport (these appear elsewhere on the form).

Fill in the section on school subjects with your **five** favourite subjects (e.g. German, History, Art).

Write in **French**.

Passetemps	*Matières Préférées*
1 _____	1 _____
2 _____	2 _____
3 _____	3 _____
4 _____	4 _____
5 _____	5 _____

(10)

MEG 1993

Examiner's tip A simple list question. This should cause no problems, but read the instructions carefully and note that sports are not to be included.

WRITING L

During your holiday in France in an isolated village a French neighbour who is going to shop in a large town offers to do some errands for your family. You list **in French** the following **five** errands requested by your parents (mentioning the places and what you want.) You should write 25–30 words. Full sentences are not required.

1 Post Office ... buy a stamp.
2 Theatre ... reserve seats/tickets.
3 Tourist Office ... ask for a map of the region.
4 ⎫
5 ⎬ Mention two different shops and say what your parents want from them. (20)
  ⎭

NICCEA 1994

Examiner's tip A slightly more guided list question. Notice how you are free to choose your own shops and items on the last task. No need to impress here! No need for long sentences – play safe and write French that you know is correct.

Letts

Q&A

You are staying in France. Whilst alone in the house you take a phone call for your pen-friend's mother, and write down this message in French from her sister.

> **Say** that her sister telephoned
> and that she has bought some new armchairs.
> **Ask** if she would like to see them. (6)
>
> *SEG 1993*

Examiner's tip A phone message to note. Notice that you need to use past tenses here. What will you write if you don't know the French for 'armchairs'? Think of the word which gets closest in meaning (*chaises*) or a general word like *meubles* – it's better than leaving a blank. Remember what has been said about how to write questions.

You are on holiday at a camp site in France and see this note on a board at reception.

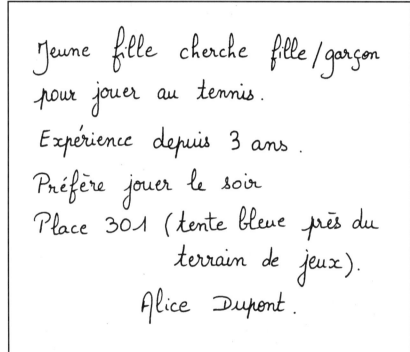

Jeune fille cherche fille/garçon
pour jouer au tennis.
Expérience depuis 3 ans.
Préfère jouer le soir
Place 301 (tente bleue près du
terrain de jeux).
Alice Dupont.

Alice is not in when you call, so you leave a note, **in French**, telling her:

— your name and age;
— which country you are from;
— you have been playing tennis for five years;
— you would like to play after 7 o'clock;
— you are in the grey caravan, opposite the shop.

Write neatly and put down all the information you are asked to give. The number of words is not important. (12)

NEAB 1994

Examiner's tip Another note, but with a stimulus in French which you can refer to for some of the words and phrases. It's alright to write the number '7' for the time, but **don't** use 'pm' – always remember to add *heures*. Remember to tick off the tasks as you complete them.

WRITING O You are going to Paris to stay with your pen-friend, Nathalie. In her last letter she includes this note from her mother.

> J'attends ta visite avec impatience mais j'ai encore certaines choses à te demander.
>
> D'abord Nathalie m'a dit qu'on mange beaucoup en Angleterre au petit déjeuner. C'est vrai? Et quels sont tes plats préférés?
>
> Et ensuite, qu'est-ce que tu veux faire pendant ton séjour? Enfin, quand vas-tu arriver à la gare du Nord?
>
> Amicalement.
> Danielle Martinez
> (La maman de Nathalie)

Write a reply to Madame Martinez, in **French**.

Tell her:
1 what you have for breakfast;
2 what foods you don't like;
3 one thing you'd like to do during your visit;
4 you are going to arrive at 3 pm, on 29th May.

Ask her:
5 what the weather is like in Paris in May;
6 what her telephone number is.

Remember to give your letter a suitable beginning and ending.

Write neatly and put down all the information you are asked to give. The number of words is not important. (12)

NEAB 1993

Examiner's tip This is the first of the letters for you to practise. This one has a French stimulus again, which you will use to help you write your letter. Be careful not to copy too closely, however – for example, in task **3** you will no doubt need to use a different verb from *faire*, used in the question to ask what you would like **to do**. Note that task **2** asks what food**s**, so mention more than one.

Before you leave the *gîte* where you have been staying during your holiday in France, your family ask you to write some comments in the visitors' book. You should write about 80 words **in French** dealing with **all** the points mentioned below.

HIGHER

WRITING P

1 Excursions que vous avez faites.
2 Ce que vous avez trouvé d'intérêt dans la région.
3 Restaurants que vous avez visités.
4 Les marchés que vous avez visités et les courses que vous avez faites là. (18)

NICCEA 1992

Examiner's tip This is a task where you are required to use the past tense to write of your impressions of a holiday area. You need to follow the points outlined, obviously, but you also need to use your initiative to give details of the restaurants, the markets and so on. Remember that you will use the imperfect tense to describe what things were like.

You receive this letter from a new pen-friend. You write to her **in French**. Include the following points and any other relevant material to make sure you write a full 100 words:

WRITING Q

— say you would like to do an exchange visit
— answer the **four** questions Magali asks in the letter.

> Villeneuve, le 4 octobre 94.
> Salut!
> C'est moi ta nouvelle correspondante. J'ai quinze ans et j'habite à la campagne près de Villeneuve. Au collège, en ce moment, j'ai beaucoup de travail. Quelles matières préfères-tu?
> Que fais-tu pendant ton temps libre? Moi, je joue de la batterie. As-tu des frères ou des soeurs? Qu'est-ce que tu as fait pendant les grandes vacances?
> Ecris-moi vite,
> Amitiés,
> Magali.

(20)

MEG 1994

Examiner's tip In this informal letter, you can again make use of the stimulus material. Be sure to answer all four questions asked in the letter as well as dealing with the first task and, as always, writing a suitable opening and ending to your letter.

Your French teacher has arranged a week's work-experience in Paris for you. You have just received this letter.

Hôtel Beauséjour,
10, Avenue Wagram,
75008 Paris.

15.05.92

Cher Monsieur/Mademoiselle,

C'est avec plaisir que nous vous offrons un poste dans notre hôtel pendant une durée d'une semaine.

Comme il s'agit de la première fois que nous employons un(e) Anglais(e), nous désirerions en savoir un peu plus à votre sujet: votre personnalité, votre niveau en français....

Pourriez-vous également nous faire savoir si vous voulez travailler à la Réception, au restaurant, au bar, au club des sports de l'hôtel ou en chambres?

Si vous avez la moindre question à nous poser, n'hésitez pas à me contacter.

Veuillez agréer, Monsieur/Mademoiselle, l'expression de mes sentiments distingués,

A. Berenguer.

Anny Berenguer.
Direction.

Write a reply, **in French**, to Madame Berenguer, thanking her for her letter.

Tell her about:
— your personal qualities;
— your knowledge of French and any other foreign languages.

Describe any previous experience you have had of working with others in or outside school. Answer her question about where in the hotel you wish to work **and** give a reason.

Ask her:
— what hours you will have to work;
— if you will be living in the hotel.

Finally, say how you feel about working in France.

Write neatly and put down **all** the information you are asked to give. The number of words is not important.

(12)

NEAB 1992

Examiner's tip This gives you a formal letter to practise. The important thing here is to read all instructions and stimulus material carefully, ticking off each point as you deal with it. Since it states that the number of words is unimportant, you can concentrate on communicating all the points in a simple and, as far as possible, a correct way, referring where it helps to the stimulus letter. Note that you have to give a **reason** on one of the tasks.

Write in French a composition of about 100 words. Credit will be given for using a wide variety of words and expressions, but irrelevant material will earn no marks.

You should be able to complete the task in about 100 words but if you use more you will not be penalised. You are strongly advised not to exceed the limit by a wide margin.

While you were in France, you and your French friend witnessed a minor accident, and you were both asked to give your names as possible witnesses even though no one was seriously hurt.

You decide to write down your version of events in case you are asked for a statement. Give details, including the weather, time of day, description of the vehicles, and anything else you think relevant.

Make use of the sketch your friend drew, which is shown below.

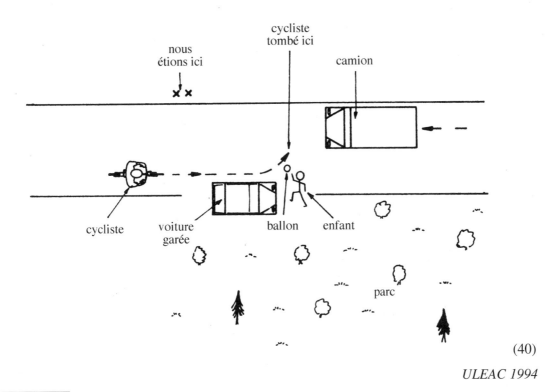

(40)

ULEAC 1994

Examiner's tip The topic of accidents often comes up and this is an example where you have witnessed an accident in France. Plan the essay carefully before you start. You need to know verbs such as *courir, renverser, heurter* or *entrer en collision, déraper, se blesser* etc. Note the suggestions given for enhancing your account and use words given in the sketch.

Imagine that the events in the pictures below happened to you. Write an account **in French of 100–120 words** about the incident to a French friend.

(80)

WJEC 1994

(i)    (ii)

(iii)    (iv)

> **Examiner's tip** Although not all Exam Boards use the series of pictures as stimulus material, they provide useful examples for practising your written French. The instructions state that the events **happened** to you. Therefore you must use the past tenses. Use the perfect for completed actions *(je suis arrivé(e)*; *j'ai lu*; and *j'ai remarqué* are examples you might use in this account), and the imperfect tense for scene-setting, description and explaining what was going on (e.g. *c'était vendredi*; *il faisait chaud*; *pendant que ma soeur payait l'addition*). It would be good to use the pluperfect tense as well; in picture (iii) you could write *j'ai remarqué que quelqu'un **avait** volé...* (**had** stolen).

Your pen-friend's school magazine is producing an issue on travel and transport. He/she asks you to write an account of a journey you have made by public transport in Great Britain. Give your personal impressions and include enough detail on the travelling, your fellow-passengers, reasons for the journey, etc. to make sure you write the full 150 words. Write **in French**.

(20)

MEG 1994

| Examiner's tip | This final example, like the last one in Part 1, gives you practice in writing about impressions and reasons have to be included. Make sure you have learned phrases to give opinions like *à mon avis*, *je crois que* and so on, which were mentioned at the end of Part 1 of this section. Notice, however, that this question asks you to write about a journey that you **have made**, so it is a past tense narrative as well as an exercise in expressing opinions and reasons. |

Answers

This section provides answers for the Listening and Reading exercises in this book.

LISTENING ANSWERS

Task	Answer	Mark
A 1	5.	1
2	Free/nothing.	1
3	Pay at the cash desk.	1
4	8 fr 50.	1
5	It's too big.	1

Examiner's tip You won't have had much trouble with these, but remember to learn thoroughly simple basics such as numbers. On Q.3, 'pay in cash' is wrong – listen carefully and you hear *à la caisse*. On Q.5, 'it's big' or 'it's very big' would not be sufficient – you need to show understanding of *trop*.

Task	Answer	Mark
B 1	Chips; pancakes; ice-creams (any two).	2
2	First floor (upstairs) and turn left.	2
3	Tomorrow.	1
4	Wednesday.	1
5	Ham; one day (today only).	2

Examiner's tip Don't answer with a French word! (it's surprisingly easily done) so don't use *crêpes* on Q.1. Make sure you learn the days of the week (Q.4) – they come up in each exam and are easy marks as long as you know them! Be on the look-out for questions which indicate two marks; it's usually obvious because two separate answers will be required, but it's a good idea to put a circle round the (2) during your reading time so that you can be sure you don't overlook it.

Task	Answer	Mark
C	(a) History	1
	(b) Art	1
	(c) Maths	1
	(d) French	1
	(e) Chemistry	1
	Tuesday is not too bad.	1

Examiner's tip If you listen carefully to her opinion, there are several pointers to the right answer, but listen carefully to it all before making your choice and always check during the second listening.

Task	Answer	Mark
D 1	Bus station.	1
2	Thursday evening at 8 o'clock.	1

You need to hear more than simply *gare* to answer the first question correctly. Note the wording of the second one. Whenever a question contains the word 'exactly', you know that a fairly detailed answer is needed (even though there is only one mark available).

Task	Answer	Mark
E 1	(a) foggy	1
	(b) nice and sunny	1
	(c) 18 degrees	1
	(d) wind	1

Weather is an important topic to revise. Be careful to pick out the right temperature on Q.(c) – it's **not** the first one you hear. Note also that the material for the answers does not come in the order of the questions.

Task	Answer	Mark
2	(a) **C**	1
	(b) **D**	1
	(c) **B**	1
	(d) **A**	1
	(e) **E**	1

Learn the less common weather expressions, like *averses* (Q.(c)), *orages* (Q.(d)) and *gelées* (Q.(e)). Learn to recognise words based on roots you know such as *ensoleillé* (based on *soleil*), *froideur* (*froid*) or *chaleur* (*chaud*).

Task	Answer	Mark
F 1	(In order from left, top row): bathroom; her bedroom; kitchen (In order, bottom row): bedroom; lounge/living room	5
2	(a) garage: old.	1
	(b) garden: long; with vegetables; with a tree	3

Make sure you know your *droite* from your *gauche*!

Task	Answer	Mark
G 1	North of France, near Belgian border.	1
2	It was grey; it was dirty; it rained a lot. (any two)	2
3	Wanted to be a doctor or a film star.	2
4	When she was at journalist's school in Paris.	1

Task	Answer	Mark
5	700 days.	1
H 1	Have a game of tennis.	1
2	He's working.	1
3	She has asked Annette's brother to play because she likes him.	2
4	Went to cinema with Annette's brother.	2
5	He's silly.	1

Examiner's tip Note that questions **3** and **4** carry two marks, so listen for more than one detail. You may have a problem in locating the answer to **3** if you don't know the verb for 'to blush', but with careful listening you will hear *tu deviens toute rouge*.

Task	Answer	Mark
I 1	E	1
2	D	1
3	B	1
4	A	1
5	C	1

Examiner's tip Key words give you the answers, but you must listen to the whole extract before you decide. Beware of the traps! For instance, the second extract mentions the weather at the start, but it turns out to be traffic report. The weather is also mentioned in the last extract, which is in fact a sports report.
Note how recognition of the future tense (*il y aura*; *commencera*) helps give the answer for Q.4.

Task	Answer	Mark
J 1	(i) There is a strike and there will be no ferry departures that evening.	2
	(ii) Take a ferry from Roscoff – they can change the ticket.	1
2 (a)	(i) Angrily.	1
	(ii) Roscoff is a long way away – they can't walk there!	1
	(iii) He's sorry, but they can't do anything about it. He says that there is a bus for Roscoff.	2
	(iv) To telephone the English family.	1
(b)	Everything will be alright – there will be no problems. The English parents have been told about the situation. Don't forget to telephone us as soon as you can.	3

Task		Answer	Mark

Examiner's tip Note the mark allocation – there are three marks for the last question, so you can expect to hear three separate things said. Although you can never rely on guesswork, you can sometimes work out the answer by understanding a certain amount of the French and using your intelligence to formulate a full answer (this is one example of 'gist understanding'). Note that you can get an idea of the reaction of the speaker through the tone of voice.

K	**1**		Prepares the plans according to the client's wishes.	1
	2		Roof repairs OR central heating installation.	1
	3	(a)	Make repairs to a castle.	1
		(b)	The castle dates from the 17th century, so he had to do everything in the style of that period.	2
	4		Pleased.	1

Examiner's tip Q.4: although he was nervous at the prospect of a difficult job, the feeling about being asked to do it was pleasure. With these multiple-choice questions, always be on the look out for those alternatives designed to trap you!

L	**1**	(a)	It was difficult to further his career as a pianist as he wanted (in freedom).	1
		(b)	It has become more humane. It is going in the right direction.	2
	2	(a)	His first piano teacher.	1
		(b)	She was 103 years old. She told him off for not having written to her during his exile.	2
	3	(a)	To make films in Russia.	1
		(b)	Nothing.	1

Examiner's tip Note the use of *bon(ne)* to mean 'right' in *la bonne direction* – if you wrote 'the good direction' it would not be accepted. In the same way, you need a suitable rendering of *réaliser* (not 'to realise') and you should note the special use of *tourner* for making a film.

Be careful how you write your answers to these Higher Level questions. Write enough to show that you have understood, but make sure your English is clear and unambiguous – examiners have to distinguish between those candidates who really understand the French and those who have simply made an intelligent guess.

M	**1**	For phoning so late.	1
	2	Her daughter.	1
	3	Continuous vomiting.	1
	4	Same as last time.	1
	5	Tomorrow at 6 pm.	1

Listening answers

Task	Answer	Mark

> **Examiner's tip** Wait until the second listening to answer – it's easy to mishear and write 'aspirin' for **Q.4** (the point is that she must NOT give aspirin). In the same way, although she hopes the doctor can visit in the morning, she finds out that he can't come until the evening.

Task	Answer	Mark
N 1	His boss and an American.	2
2	Husband shouldn't feel obliged to invite boss to dinner; she doesn't know what to serve an American for dinner – she doesn't want to serve American food.	2
3	Three years.	1
4	That he has learned to eat French food.	1
5	Saturday; the husband can help with the housework.	2

> **Examiner's tip** Two marks on **Q.1** will mean two people, but listen carefully – you first assume, like the speaker, that it will be the boss and his wife. Don't write down the first day you hear for **Q.5**.

Task	Answer	Mark
O (a)	Needs to be in Calais by mid-day; otherwise he might miss the ferry; English friends are waiting for him at Dover; he can't contact them.	3
(b)	Farmers.	1
(c)	They should take their case to the government rather than troubling the holiday makers.	3

> **Examiner's tip** (a) With three marks available, write down all that you understand – there are four possible answers, so three of them would be enough for full marks, but don't guess if you are not sure of the meaning. Don't forget the verb *manquer* – 'to miss', and remember then the French call Dover *Douvres* (as they call London *Londres*). (c) Although there are again three marks available, there are not three separate details. This is where you draw your conclusion about why the traffic is at a standstill; the point is that the farmers are making a protest by blocking the road.

Task	Answer	Mark
P 1	Hope.	1
2	1½ years.	1
3	Their foster/new families.	1
4	She will always welcome them; she is sorry for them.	1
5	Eating rice.	1
6	She could never refuse to help a child; she already has three children of her own.	1
7	Many other children remain in a serious situation in Bangladesh.	1

Task	Answer		Mark

READING ANSWERS

Task		Answer	Mark
A	1	Push.	1
	2	Furniture.	1
	3	Shoes.	1

Examiner's tip As a sign on a gate, 'push' would be quite a logical answer anyway. Don't forget to learn shop names, and learn the difference between *chaussures* and *chaussettes*!

B	1	Entrée.	1
	2	Boucherie.	1

Examiner's tip Don't confuse *boucherie* (butcher's) with *boulangerie* (baker's)!

C	1	Peas; mushrooms.	2
	2	Sea food.	1
	3	A birth.	1

Examiner's tip Don't forget *fruits de mer* meaning 'sea food' (Q.**2**). Because it is so easily taken to mean 'fruits', it's a favourite with examination setters!

D	(a)	Leather.	1
	(b)	(i) Prices (ii) Choice.	2
	(c)	Sunday.	1
	(d)	7 pm.	1

Task	Answer	Mark

| **E** | (a) 390 francs. | 1 |
| | (b) Nothing (it's free). | 1 |

| **F** | (a) Edinburgh airport. On Tuesday 26th July. | 3 |
| | (b) Go on walks (trips) in the mountains; see the Loch Ness monster; eat Scottish specialities such as salmon. | 3 |

G	(a) A fortnight.	1
	(b) On the South coast.	2
	(c) People got up.	1
	(d) Had to help do the washing-up and prepare lunch.	3
	(e) Three or four times.	1
	(f) Pottery; horse riding.	2
	(g) 500 metres.	1
	(h) Shopping.	1

H	(a) Dad is sleeping.	1
	(b) To the book shop in the Rue St. Jacques.	1
	(c) Quite late that evening.	1
	(d) Meet Mark in front of the bus station.	2
	(e) To repair the TV.	1
	(f) In the cupboard to the right of the washing machine.	3

Task		Answer	Mark
I	**1**	Driving lessons for people from age 16.	2
	2	Your portrait drawn by computer.	1

Examiner's tip With two marks available and two lines for the answer, give a full and complete answer for question **1**.

J	(a)	You've danced all night.	2
	(b)	Onion soup.	2
	(c)	You will still manage to go jogging.	1
	(d)	The first of January.	1

Examiner's tip In (d), don't be fooled by seeing particular dates given (23rd September etc.). You get the answer by understanding *ce premier jour de l'année*.

K		Rest for a few hours. Have a light meal. Take no alcohol or drugs that could cause drowsiness.	3

Examiner's tip Given the context of a road safety leaflet and the inclusion of *boisson alcoolisée*, you could make a sensible conclusion about the nature of this advice, even though some of the vocabulary in the item is quite tricky.

L	(a)	305,447.	1
	(b)	Agriculture/wine producing.	1
	(c)	Mild and dry.	2
	(d)	(i) The variety of the countryside (sea, mountains etc.).	
		(ii) Exceptional cultural history.	2
	(e)	It mentions the necessary road maps.	1

Examiner's tip Notice how many of the words are similar in French and English. Once you look carefully at text and questions, the exercise is not that difficult. But don't rush into it – pick the correct number for the population in (a), for instance, and not the first number that you see (which is for its area).

M	(a)	4.	1
	(b)	Plane.	1
	(c)	They have to go somewhere else because the person they were to meet in Dallas isn't there.	2
	(d)	The person has left them a message.	1

Task		Answer	Mark
	(e)	The weather forecast.	1
N 1		G	1
2		B	1
3		C	1
4		H	1
5		A	1
6		B	1

Examiner's tip Looking for key words is not always enough. The word *amis* for instance, appears in both G and H. This may help, however, in narrowing down the options. Notice how familiarity with the future tense, always used a lot in horoscopes, is a great help to understanding. Did you read the instruction carefully and note that one letter could be used more than once? This was the case for questions **2** and **6**.

O		The advertisement talks about Sunday trading. It says that cinemas are free to open on a Sunday (along with museums and theatres) but not bookshops and record shops. Clearly the message is that this is unfair.	2

P		You could have made any four of the following points:	

1 Nurses have gone on strike for the fifth time since September.
2 Doctors and most hospital workers have joined in.
3 When they demonstrated in October, tear gas and water canon were used to keep them away from the President's Palace and two nurses were injured.
4 The public were angry about this because nurses are not militant.
5 The nurses are going to continue to demonstrate for better pay, which is at present very low.

4

Examiner's tip Read the text through slowly several times. Make notes on what you understand. Use your knowledge of what you understand and your general comprehension of the gist of the article to write down your four important points, trying to make your answers as full and readable as you can.

Q 1		He's funny (amusing); he's nice (kind); he's sensitive.	3
2	(i)	Laughed at her (made fun of her).	1
	(ii)	Drop him (leave him).	1
3		She is afraid of hurting him.	1
4		They want to show their friends they have the best-looking boy.	1

Task	Answer	Mark
5	If Sandra went out with him because she dare not say no.	1

Examiner's tip There is much useful vocabulary here of the sort that often comes up in Higher Level exercises. Be sure to learn the vocabulary of emotion – words like *ému*, *amoureux*, *désespéré* and don't forget that *sensible* means 'sensitive'.

Task	Answer	Mark
R (a)	Almost 6 million people speak French there.	1
(b)	It's very cold. Sometimes in January the temperature falls to minus 35 degrees. There are heavy falls of snow up to 1 or 1½ metres deep or even 2 metres in the North.	2
(c)	She is his wife. She hasn't come with him to England, but she will visit him at Christmas.	3
(d)	The children of his father and his second wife.	2

Examiner's tip When there are several marks for a question, write as much as you understand from the text which directly answers the question. Your answers need to be a precise rendering of the text – hence simply '6 million' is not an exact answer for (a). In the same way, look carefully for the exact temperature for (b) – it's very easy to overlook the vital *sous zéro*. In (c), you need to recognise the future tense of the irregular verb *venir* in order to give a precise answer to the third part.

Task	Answer	Mark
S	The campsite owner thanks you for the cheque which he has received and confirms your reservation for a pitch from the 8th to the 16th of August.	2

Examiner's tip Once you have deciphered the writing and thought carefully about the context of this letter (having read the question carefully) it is not too difficult to understand what has been written.

Task	Answer	Mark
T (a)	Anger/disbelief at people's heartlessness.	1
(b)	Their treatment of their pets; abandoning them when they go on holiday.	2
(c)	The fire brigade.	1
(d)	Those aged 6 months, born in February, and just reaching maturity.	2
(e)	They are too noisy and energetic and therefore become too awkward to take on holiday.	2
(f)	It's easier to let them free than to kill them at birth.	2
(g)	They often move house and can't look after them properly any longer.	2
(h)	They make use of kennels for their pets when they go on holiday.	1
(i)	They lose them and then go back home.	2

Task	Answer	Mark

Examiner's tip These answers are perhaps longer than would be required to be awarded the marks, but it is worth including as much information as you can understand as long as it seems relevant to the question. At the same time, as was mentioned in the opening hints to the Reading section, do be wary of including incorrect information which could result in the marks being witheld.

A final point about the answers given to these exercises: the questions can be answered using a number of different words. Examiners want to see that you have understood the concepts in the text, but they must be confident that your answer shows true understanding of the French. Always remember, then, to re-read your answers and ask yourself if they are clear and unambiguous and make it obvious to the examiner that you have understood the French.